F·R·E·E
TO
DISAGREE

F·R·E·E
TO
DISAGREE

Moving Beyond the Arguments
Over Christian Liberty

John Wecks

kregel
RESOURCES

Grand Rapids, MI 49501

Free to Disagree: Moving Beyond the Arguments Over Christian Liberty

© 1996 by John Wecks

Published by Kregel Resources, an imprint of Kregel Publications, P.O. Box 2607, Grand Rapids, MI 49501. Kregel Resources provides timely and relevant resources for Christian life and service. Your comments and suggestions are valued.

Cover photo: Frank Herholdt / Tony Stone Images
Cover design: Alan G. Hartman
Book design: Nicholas G. Richardson

Library of Congress Cataloging-in-Publication Data
Wecks, John, 1949–
    Free to disagree: moving beyond the arguments over Christian liberty / by John Wecks.
        p.   cm.
    1. Christian ethics. 2. Liberty of conscience. I. Title.
BJ1231.W43   1996   241—dc20   95-38413
                                                                    CIP
ISBN 0-8254-3954-x

1 2 3 4 5 printing/year 00 99 98 97 96

Printed in the United States of America

To the students of
Multnomah Biblical Seminary
and
other members of the body of Christ
who have encouraged me to write

Table of Contents

Foreword

DISSENT WAS BORN in Eden when Adam and Eve decided to disbelieve God, and opposition has flourished ever since. In our times the church of Christ has been ravaged with increasing discord. Although believers claim to know the God of peace and love, we have demanded the right of free speech and proceeded to bash each other in hypocritical, free-for-all fashion.

Christian leaders, of all people, should exemplify Christlike forbearance and patience. Instead, some stand stubbornly in the path to harmony while others argue over the best road to get there. When disagreement becomes heated and emotions run high, we need the Bible's advice on making wise decisions. Churches and church leaders need less heat and more scriptural illumination.

John Wecks writes to shine more light on the sometimes rough road to deeper and stronger relationships. *Free to Disagree* dares to step into the fracas of controversy over countless issues to provide road signs for healthy travel toward Christlikeness. The book asks everyone in the debate to stop arguing long enough to look to God's Word for an attitude check. The author points to the atlas of God's Word in order to find the best route for all travelers.

A professor of Bible study methods and homiletics, John combines inductive Bible study skills with a passion to communicate the Bible in fresh ways. As a pastor he teaches awareness and sensitivity to others.

Each of us holds opinions about gray areas of Christian behavior; this is God's plan. We are overdue, however, for this thoughtful and helpful road map to conflict resolution. Sometimes the path is bumpy because we can't agree, but this much-needed book encourages us to join hands with good attitudes on the way.

Howard G. Hendricks
Distinguished Professor and Chairman
Center for Christian Leadership
Dallas Theological Seminary

Acknowledgments

THE LORD IS to be praised for the way his Word has spoken so powerfully and practically to my heart, life, and ministry through the years. If I weren't firmly convinced of the relevancy of his Word, this book would not have been written.

I also want to acknowledge the many godly people who have had an impact on my life. Some of the concepts and principles in this book reflect a lifetime of exposure to various teachers. Other parts of the book were developed through opportunities to present this material in the classroom and in various churches and conferences since 1984.

Two groups were especially helpful in the process of writing the book. The adult class at Laurelwood Baptist Church in Vancouver, Washington, allowed me to teach these concepts for twelve weeks. Many members of the class read the early manuscript and provided helpful insight. One deacon, Bob DeViney, carefully evaluated my early efforts.

A second group is my students. Feedback from students at Southeastern Bible College came in our discussions on the book of Romans. More good insight came from the students in my Conflict Resolution class at Multnomah Biblical Seminary, a class I have taught every year since 1988. The lively class interaction, the refinement of ideas, and the good discussion had a direct impact on this book. Coral Hilby, M.D., was particularly helpful in those portions she had time to review with care and skill.

I thank my wife, Carley, and my daughters, Joy and Jenny, for the help they gave me during the writing of the book. I thank them, too, for letting me use illustrations from our lives together as a family. The names and characters discussed in the book do not represent any specific individuals and are fictional depictions for illustration of the issues only.

I also wish to thank Dennis Hillman and the editorial staff at Kregel Publications for working with me to publish the book.

Unless otherwise noted, Scripture quotations are from the *New International Version*.

Many people helped in the writing of this book, and I gratefully acknowledge their many helpful and positive contributions; the final responsibility for its contents, however, is mine.

Introduction

GOD MIGHT POST a sign over the front door of several churches—Ichabod, an Old Testament name which means "no glory." The light of God's glory grows dim when believers argue endlessly over such issues as budgets, hiring staff, changes in curriculum, building programs, fund raising, or the style of worship. Controversies can surface in any situation—at congregational, board, and committee meetings; at Bible studies; in the parking lot after church; and in homes.

Those who love Jesus Christ, who turn to the Scriptures for answers, often come away from heated discussions with rising blood pressure, frustration, and disappointment, wondering if the Bible really has any practical help for the myriad of issues they face. I believe it does.

This book is written to guide Christians toward spiritual health and beauty through the wise application of biblical principles in morally neutral matters and through personal decisions which reflect purity, maintain unity, and build up others spiritually. These goals are in danger of extinction in many areas of the evangelical church today.

What grieves me most is the unhealthy conflict prevalent in many churches today. Frequently, conflicts occur over personalities, opinions, philosophies, methods, styles, traditions, peripheral doctrines, or other nonessentials. The simple truth is that most of these issues are not worth fighting over.

In one sense divisive problems shouldn't be a surprise. Many specific objects, behaviors, ideas, and methods within a particular culture are not clearly addressed in the Bible. Individuals develop

13

their own opinions regarding these issues and often hold to them strongly. I believe the Bible allows us to hold differing opinions in these areas. Unfortunately, unhealthy conflict often erupts in our churches when attitudes turn sour toward other Christians who disagree with majority opinion. The cause of Christ is hindered when damaged, broken churches do not seek reconciliation. The mishandling of disputable matters continues to split churches, devastate relationships, and weaken the body of Christ.

Part of my mission is preventative in nature. My desire is to help churches remain healthy by avoiding disunity over cultural issues where the Scriptures seem to allow a variety of opinion. Many of the principles spring from the course I have taught at Multnomah Biblical Seminary entitled "Conflict Resolution in the Church." However, this is not a book about conflict management in the broadest sense. This book focuses on biblically neutral concerns or disputable matters. Very few books related to conflict management or the theology of conflict address the current questions raised by the exhortations in Romans 14–15 and in 1 Corinthians 8–10. I have been surprised by the lack of material to assist Christians with practical, daily decisions in neutral areas. I have written this book, therefore, to use the powerful principles of God's Word to address the contemporary, cultural issues which sometimes divide our churches.

Christians zealous for holy living often confuse personal convictions and corporate traditions with God's commandments. Traditions of the church are revered sometimes as though they are equivalent to God's law. For example, some Christians believe that the old hymns are more acceptable for worship than the newer choruses. One gets the impression from some church-goers that the traditional order of worship or the method of administering the ordinances cannot be changed or altered without sin. Cultural norms such as length of hair, style of dress, food and drink, or types of recreation are sometimes used to define what pleases God. When cultural norms begin to change, some of these same Christians consider the shift to be a corruption of God's moral standards. Few of us continually monitor social issues to assist each other in differentiating between the cultural or traditional and the moral or biblical.

How many well-meaning church members are on the brink of ignoring God's Word in order to maintain a church-made facade of holiness? American Christianity disputes the type of music appropriate for worship while church members gossip, lie, and generally ignore pre-marital sex and adultery between its members. Jesus' indictment leaps off the biblical page with a disturbing relevance: "You have a fine way of setting aside the commands of God in order to observe your own traditions!" (Mark 7:9).

With Scripture as our foundation, this book will be a lively discussion of life-changing principles to govern decisions in the domain of neutral things. Because God's Word is our database, the style interacts between the Bible and contemporary life. Unless the content of this book is rooted in the transforming truth of God's Word, it would have little effectiveness and be a futile endeavor.

My focus will be on the healthy application of our liberty in Christ. Therefore we will be more conformed to the image of Christ in the way we respond when we disagree with other Christians in the area of morally neutral things. The book avoids slipping into a list of do's and don'ts which might abort freedom in Jesus Christ. For this reason, you might be frustrated with the lack of enough cautions for those who tend to abuse their liberty. We do need, of course, Paul's caution: "You, my brothers, were called to be free. But do not use your freedom to indulge the sinful nature; rather, serve one another in love" (Gal. 5:13).

Because of the danger of generalization and the potential to be misunderstood, the first few chapters amplify concepts *without answering every question or balancing every truth.* Wary readers might feel early chapters encourage license to sin but nothing could be further from my desire. Some readers may want statements to balance the early principles. I have chosen to allow later chapters to equalize the message of the book.

The book is also designed to help the reader understand his or her own feelings, emotions, and convictions. It will encourage readers to place a higher priority on right attitudes toward others who disagree.

Because the content touches issues very close to the core of an individual's most personal convictions, some readers may experience an emotional reaction—deep passions might trigger a reaction to defend long-held convictions. The potential for a strong response to this book both scares and satisfies me. On the one hand, I'm afraid that some readers might angrily set the book aside, and I instantly lose credibility with them. On the other hand, I'm satisfied to know that many readers will identify their own emotional responses as a key element in understanding how to manage differences with other Christians.

We may be able to look objectively at disagreements over concerns which do not matter to us personally. When we feel strongly about an issue, however, we have moved into the very arena where the principles of the book become most helpful—and the application of the book becomes most difficult.

This book does not develop an exhaustive list of principles for the spiritual life or for holy living in general, although the concepts do encourage holy, relational living. Nor is this a book designed to help determine the will of God in all decisions. Its main focus is on the dozens of decisions that believers face in biblically neutral areas.

My goal is that readers be able to understand whether they are "weak" or "strong" in relation to a specific issue and be able to respond with godly attitudes toward others who disagree with their personal convictions.

May God be pleased to use this book to help you discern essentials from nonessentials, the moral from the immoral, the biblical from the cultural, God's laws from human traditions, the wise from the unwise, the useful from the useless, and the beneficial from the damaging. May the Lord use the book to help members of local churches maintain the unity of the Spirit in the bond of peace. Let's learn how to disagree agreeably in the huge arena of neutral things.

> In essentials, unity;
> In nonessentials, liberty;
> In all things, charity.
> —Martin Luther

— *1* —

Falling Off the Neutral Fence

Pastor George waited for his staff to arrive for the Tuesday meeting. After they had assembled, Bill, a retired pastor who helped part-time, spoke up. "Did you see what Chip Thomas's daughter did Sunday morning?"

George responded, "No, I guess I didn't."

"She walked right into the worship service wearing slacks. I can understand it on a visitor perhaps—but not on one of our members."

"Hmmm." George waited to hear what else had happened.

Bill continued. "I decided to talk to Chip about it."

"How did he respond?" George asked.

"He seemed upset with me," said Bill, still obviously offended by the incident. "Young people today have no respect for the Lord!"

The staff meeting went on, but the impact remained. For Pastor Bill the issue was not fashion taste but moral conviction.

❖   ❖   ❖

Marilyn, in a telephone conversation with Sue, complained about the use of drums in the previous Sunday morning's worship service. "There's absolutely no reason for it," she said. "Drums should be left in the night clubs and dance halls. The beat is sensuous and totally out of place in a solemn worship service."

"Oh, really? I'm sorry you feel that way," Sue said. "I liked it. I thought they really brought life to our expressions of worship and praise to God." Sue was hoping Marilyn wouldn't discourage the pastoral staff. "Marilyn, you need to get rid of your judgmental attitude about this. I see nothing wrong with them."

❖   ❖   ❖

Christians disagree. How do we decide who is right and who is wrong? In both of the scenarios above, the issues do not necessarily carry moral consequences. They are areas of Christian liberty since the Bible does not clearly teach anything against women's wearing slacks tailored for women or drums being played in morning worship.[1] The Bible does not indicate one person's opinion is wrong and another's is right. The Bible does, however, encourage Christians to hold personal convictions based both on their understanding of the Bible and their own background (Rom. 14:5, 22). A person may even base his or her conviction on biblical principles such as modesty and appropriateness. However, the means by which we apply principles of modesty and appropriateness are culturally based. What one believer considers to be modest or appropriate may be different from what another person believes.[2] Dilemmas sometimes arise when these differing believers try to work together toward a common position. Such issues are sometimes called neutral issues.

What exactly is a neutral issue? A neutral issue is anything that the Bible does not clearly say is either right or wrong but that someone could hold as wrong based on personal conviction. Paul says in Romans 14:14, "I know and am convinced in the Lord Jesus that nothing is unclean in itself [that is, certain things are morally neutral in themselves] but to him who thinks anything to be unclean, to him it is unclean" (NASB). When a person doubts whether God allows a debated practice or item, he or she is unable to freely participate without feeling as though that action is a sin. For them, it is doubtful whether God approves; therefore, the matter is "disputable." Paul refers to these issues in Romans 14:1 when he says, "Accept him whose faith is weak, without passing judgment on disputable matters."

At the same time, another Christian may see nothing wrong with the same issue and feel complete freedom before God to participate, thus being free to practice what some describe as Christian liberty or Christian freedom. The Bible is clear that material objects such as drums or women's slacks are never "wrong" in themselves, that is, as a material object (Mark 7:18–23; Rom. 14:14). Is a desk right or wrong? What about a car? A microwave oven? A switchblade? A cigar? A videotape? Someone may feel that the switchblade is wrong or maybe the cigar. Yet, the object itself has no moral value. Some of these objects may be used in the wrong way, and used wrongly an object can be a tool for sin. But by itself, an object does not have moral value.

The same is true of some actions. Is it wrong to jog? Does the Bible forbid word processing? What about other actions such as observing Christmas, shaving, shopping, playing rock music, dating (for unmarried persons of course!), women's participating in worship services, or lifting hands in worship services? One may have a strong personal conviction regarding one or more of these issues, but the Bible does not clearly address these specific actions. As a result, Christians disagree.

Many conscientious Christian people believe that the Bible gives the answer to every instance of how to please God, even if the instance is not directly mentioned. Such respect for the authority of God's Word should be encouraged, but not to the detriment of what the Bible actually teaches about questionable areas. As we will see in our study of neutral issues, the Bible teaches that two Christians can differ about an issue and both be right.

The principle of neutral issues also applies to doctrinal disagreement in areas of nonessentials. One of the first questions we have to address is what is essential and what is nonessential in matters of Christian living, philosophy of ministry, or doctrine. We often have disagreements about even the issues on which we can disagree!

How do we determine whether an issue is essential? The following five guidelines can help one determine what is essential.

1. Is it a direct, scriptural statement of command, prohibition, or exhortation?
2. Is it a biblically consistent truth derived from the compilation of scriptural evidence and interpreted by sound principles of a normal, literary interpretation?
3. Is it a normative, scriptural standard to accept or pattern to follow?
4. Is it a teaching that has generally been accepted by the church across cultural and denominational lines throughout history?
5. Is it a belief or conviction that you would die for rather than renounce as untrue for the universal body of Christ?

The fifth guideline is often the decisive one. If a person were put in front of a firing squad and directed to give up a certain personal conviction or die, that person's list of essentials would probably shrink rather quickly. What we think is important may not be so important after all.

Some doctrines are foundational to basic Christianity such as the deity of Christ or salvation by faith alone. Christians who believe God's Word have no doubt about the rightness or wrongness of actions such as murder or adultery. Gossip, lying, slander, lust, stealing, and drunkenness are also actions condemned by God although they are often tolerated by Christians today.

What about those areas where the Bible gives us freedom, however? In these areas Christians should be free to disagree agreeably. What are some of these areas? At the risk of being condemned by someone's personal conviction, each item appears on the list below because at least one Christian is convinced that it is wrong for Christians.

As you read the list, you might wonder whether some of them should be further defined, and you might think of others that you would add to the list. My opinion is that almost every item needs further description and definition and that the list is only a start on many other areas and concerns which could be added. This list serves to "jump start" our thinking about neutral issues. *Inclusion of any item should not be construed as an endorsement or disapproval.* My request is that you suspend judgment about the rightness or wrongness of an item until later in the book.

- Observing Halloween
- Carving jack-o-lanterns
- Using drums in Sunday morning worship
- Working on Sundays
- Not picketing abortion clinics
- Women wearing slacks to Sunday worship
- Men growing long hair
- Eating or drinking certain things
- Serving communion bread with leaven
- Dancing among Christians
- Not having a mid-week prayer meeting
- Moving worship time to Friday night
- Chewing tobacco
- Not observing foot washing as an ordinance
- Refusing to home school children
- Having pictures of Jesus on the wall
- Not taking an offering by passing a receptacle
- Carrying life or health insurance
- Remarrying after divorce
- Lifting hands in worship
- Not having a senior pastor

Portions of such a list change throughout the years within any given culture. Views on these same issues are often very different in other countries or cultures, which alone suggests that the item is neutral rather than a biblical, moral concern valid for any society at any time.

The real issue, however, is usually an individual's emotional response that might insist that something in this list is a sin. Such opinions may indicate that the person is a "weaker brother" on that issue. To be called a weaker brother may sound degrading and upset someone who believes strongly that he has the "right" view. Some explanation of this key biblical term is therefore necessary.

The Bible uses the words *strong* and *weak* in a specific way to describe the differences among Christians in regard to neutral issues. A Christian views each neutral issue from either of two sides. Romans 14:1 instructs the strong to "accept him whose faith is weak, without passing judgment on disputable matters," thus placing responsibility on the strong Christian to accept the weak (Rom. 14:1–3). What is the difference, then, between the strong and the weak person on a given issue?

THE WEAK CHRISTIAN

The weak Christian in this context is weak both in faith and in conscience in relation to a specific issue (or issues). Christians who are weak in faith believe that if they engage in a neutral thing, they will sin. A Christian who is weak in conscience needs more than information and maturity because even an informed, knowledgeable weak conscience still will not allow a weak person the freedom to participate. For the weak, the neutral issue is a doubtful issue.

One of the most prominent misconceptions in our churches today is to equate the weaker brother with someone who is immature. The label weak *in faith* sounds like an indictment of disciples who failed to believe in the Lord and his power. In reality, a weaker brother is a Christian who, because of weakness of faith, might be influenced to sin against his conscience. Christians who say "I would never think of doing such a thing" (regarding a neutral issue) are still defined biblically as weak. If they should ever happen to do such a thing, they would violate their convictions and conscience. In the context of a neutral issue, however, to be weak in faith is not a condition to be condemned. A person can be weak in faith regarding a particular issue and still be very spiritually mature.

A weak Christian in regard to drums used in worship may not see anything wrong with going to the movies. In our opening scenario, Pastor Bill felt it was wrong for women to wear slacks in the worship service, but he had no problem with having life insurance, which some Christians consider to be wrong.

Another point of confusion over the principle of neutral issues often arises from the emotions that are involved in the discussion. A pastor who feels strongly that no woman should wear slacks in the church service is not the stronger Christian. Rather, he is a weak brother who feels a strong personal conviction. Sadly, many pastors and church leaders are actually weaker brothers. They have convinced themselves that they are stronger brothers because they have the strength to resist those questionable issues. Some of them make their personal convictions the dogma of the church and denounce those whose participation in the questionable area clashes with their nonparticipation. As we will see in the next chapter, Romans 14:1–12 teaches that God views their judgmental spirit as the true sin rather than the participation in the neutral thing. There are different types of weak Christians as well.

The Susceptible Weak Christian

Don voiced concern over the long hair that he observed on some of the young people in his church. "It's wrong," he said. When his pastor told him that the Bible does not clearly condemn long hair on men, he relaxed slightly.[3] "Why do I feel so strongly about this, pastor?" he wondered aloud.

"When you played in a heavy metal band before you became a Christian, didn't you say that you were caught up in drugs and sex and that you had long hair?" the pastor asked. "You probably associate anyone with long hair with the sin and rebelliousness of your past."

Don agreed that his pastor's insight was correct. When the pastor encouraged him to see his responsibility not to judge others who had the freedom to wear long hair, he agreed not to condemn them.

The person who is a susceptible weak Christian feels that it is wrong to participate in a doubtful area, and every Christian should think the same way. The danger for Don lies in the fact that he might let his own hair grow long before his conviction changes. If he were to do so, he would be sinning against his own conscience and would therefore be sinning against God (see Rom. 14:23).

The Knowledgeable Weak Christian

Don needs both to keep his own hair cut short and to keep from condemning others who have long hair. He is now no longer a susceptible weak Christian but rather a weaker brother whose knowledge frees him to allow others to disagree with his personal position.

Don is still a weak brother on the issue of long hair on men, but because he now knows better, he is a knowledgeable weak Christian. Spiritually mature persons with informed consciences believe that it may be wrong for them to participate in certain matters, but they also believe that not everyone who does so is wrong.

Emotions in response to these areas run deep and strong. When a person is raised to have strong convictions that certain issues are wrong, it becomes very difficult for him or her to freely participate even though the mind has become convinced that the Bible does not condemn those issues. Thus, the mind has knowledge, but the heart does not feel the freedom to go ahead.[4]

Usually a weak Christian who has both knowledge and maturity relates well with those who disagree. When this person gives up personal rights and voluntarily chooses to abstain, others may think he is a strong brother. In actuality, when someone decides not to participate in a neutral issue, he or she may be making the choice out of a personal conviction that the issue is wrong for him or her but not necessarily wrong for others.

The Legalistic Weak Christian

"I think our churches have failed to talk about sin," Carl began. "We let people get away with things and no one talks about it."

"I agree," said Jim. "Just the other day I saw some members of our church walk into a movie theater downtown."

"What's wrong with that?" Carl felt some tension since he and his wife loved to go to movies.

"Movies promote too much sex and violence," responded Jim.

"All of them?"

"Most of them. Certainly I believe we should be completely pure as Christians. I already mentioned to the pastor that some of our members go to the movies, and he said that he had heard about it, too. He is going to say something from the pulpit next week—before it gets too far out of hand."

By this time, Carl was seething inside but kept quiet for fear he would explode. The next Sunday, the pastor dealt with the issue in his sermon. He made it clear that good Christians do not go to the movie theater.

Carl and his wife had the freedom before God to enjoy certain movies. Jim and the pastor believed that they needed to protect the moral purity of the church against such sin. Well-meaning Christians, zealous for the purity of the body of Christ, sometimes confuse biblical standards with their own personal opinions.

The church certainly needs more people to be concerned for moral purity, and mature believers will carefully consider the moral content of *all* entertainment including television, videos, magazines, radio programs, or theatrical performances. We must, however, avoid trumpeting our personal opinion as more important than clear instances of sin. While the Bible says nothing about attending movies per se, it does clearly condemn the insidious grapevine of gossip that causes others to form negative opinions about those who attend movies.

Jim and the pastor were legalistic weak brothers who had a judgmental spirit toward those who disagreed with them. To compound the problem, they spread gossip about their fellow believers and then openly and verbally attacked them. It is clear from Scripture that God is more concerned about gossip and a critical spirit than he is about someone's choice to attend a movie.

The intention of purity is commendable, but legalistic, Pharisee-like attitudes prevail in too many churches. Legalism is the false idea that a policy or requirement can be rigidly imposed on unbelievers to earn salvation or on Christians to make them more spiritual. A legalistic attitude makes others feel guilty about things not specifically taught in the Bible. Usually, a list of do's and don'ts, either in the form of written rules or unwritten expectations, are dictated to others as if they are God's requirements for holy living.

Jesus discussed this danger when the Pharisees and teachers of the law challenged Jesus' disciples for not washing their hands "according to the tradition of the elders" (Mark 7:5). The pharisaical approach to spiritual life and ministry was spawned by the Pharisees, who were what we might call the "Bible-believing" sect within Judaism. They zealously guarded their personal interpretations of the Old Testament. While they professed to honor the law and protect it from corruption, they added their man-made rules to the clear statements of Scripture and demanded that others hold to their opinion about which actions were pleasing to God. Their extreme scruples over the issue of ceremonial handwashing, a tradition of the Pharisees and not a part of the law, is an indication of their misguided agenda.

Although the word *Pharisee* describes a historical group of men who opposed Jesus Christ, their attitude and approach to the spiritual life is represented today by any Christian who seeks to impose similar demands on other Christians. Some Christians act like Pharisees when they insist that their personal opinion about an extrabiblical matter is the right opinion and then treat with contempt anyone else who disagrees with them.

The pharisaical route to purity is misguided, and it actually violates the Word of God. When a person publicly presents man-made rules and requirements as though they are the commandments of God and then condemns as sinners any Christians who do not obey these rules, such a person is acting in a pharisaical manner. In that way, legalistic weaker brothers are like the Pharisees who criticize and condemn others for not agreeing with them on a disputable matter.

THE STRONG CHRISTIAN

In the Bible's discussion of neutral issues, a strong Christian is a brother or sister whose strong faith and conscience allow him or her the freedom to participate in a debated matter without sinning. Although the strong Christian has liberty, many reasons may govern his or her behavior and cause him or her to give up this freedom.

In the earlier scenario, Carl and his wife enjoyed going to the movies. They believed that God gave them the freedom to go see a good, decent movie at the theater, and their consciences did not condemn them when they went. Carl and his wife are strong Christians on this issue.

The Nonparticipating Strong Christian

Christians may decide not to participate in certain neutral issues for many different reasons. Sometimes the reason is as simple as not wanting to. In some situations they may be trying to avoid behavior that might cause another person to stumble in their Christian life. Sometimes they give up rights in order to exemplify certain values while their children are young. Other times they lovingly give up what they might enjoy out of deference to another believer's personal convictions. Still other times, believers give up certain freedoms because it is the wisest course of action in a given situation.

The danger for these nonparticipating strong Christians is when other Christians do not agree with them on the wisdom of their course of action. The strong Christians may slip into the same judgmental attitude as the weak Christians—now the area of disagreement has shifted to the ways in which Christians should limit their freedoms. Strong nonparticipating Christians who require other strong believers to give up the right to participate end up acting like legalistic, weaker Christians.

The Lovingly Participating Strong Christian

The loving participator believes that God has given us everything richly to enjoy, and thus this person occasionally exercises freedom to participate in a neutral issue—if it can be done without violating the guidelines for the healthy expression of Christian liberty (which will be examined later in this book). Perhaps this person enjoys square dancing. If other believers nearby disagree and could be hurt, this individual will give up dancing for their sake. When this Christian is alone with people who have the same conviction or opinion, then this strong believer may proceed to enjoy dancing without any sense of guilt.

The strong Christian pays close attention to relationships in order to be aware of any fellow believer who may hold a different conviction. If someone could be hurt, the loving response is to give up one's rights.

The Proudly Participating Strong Christian

A strong Christian on a neutral issue might not be either loving or mature. Some believers insist that no other Christian has the right to tell them what they can or cannot do. Sometimes these proudly participating strong Christians are looking for other Christians who disagree simply to pick an argument with them or to flaunt their freedom.

Paul has some powerful words to say to these people in Romans 14. God condemns a proud attitude, and he places the burden of responsibility on the strong to give up their rights for the sake of those who are weak (we will examine these principles in the next two chapters). Nothing could be clearer, however, than Paul's instructions to "pursue peace and the building up of one another" (Rom. 14:19 NASB).

The following charts may help summarize different possible categories of personal conviction. Although the debated subject mentioned on the charts is attending a movie at a theater, any disputable matter could be inserted and the categories remain the same.

WEAK

Definition: A weak believer is a Christian who, because of the weakness of faith and conscience, can be influenced to sin against his or her conscience.

	Issue	Conviction	Knowledge	Teachable	Attitude	Evaluation	Confusion	Conclusions	Dangers
Susceptible (immature)	Movie at theater	Wrong to participate	No	Usually	Sincere	It's wrong for others	Appears as a legalist	Everyone who does it is guilty	1) critical of others 2) doing it
Knowledgeable (mature)	Movie at theater	Wrong for self to participate	Yes	Taught	Convinced	It's not wrong for everyone	Appears strong	Not everyone who does it sins	1) doing it 2) jealousy
Pharisaical (legalist)	Movie at theater	Wrong to participate	No	No	Convinced but proud	It's wrong for others	Thinks of self as "strong"	Everyone who does it is guilty	1) critical 2) forces "legalism"

STRONG — Definition: A strong believer is a Christian whose strong faith and conscience allows him or her the freedom to participate in a neutral thing without sinning.

	Issue	Conviction	Knowledge	Teachable	Attitude	Evaluation	Confusion	Conclusions	Dangers
Non-Participating (mature)	Movie at theater	Has freedom but chooses not to	Yes	Already Taught	Convinced and loves	It's not wrong for others	Others think the person is "weak"	Not everyone who does it is guilty	1) others more spiritual if abstain 2) critical of weak
Participating (mature)	Movie at theater	Has freedom to do it	Yes	Usually	Convinced and loves	It's not wrong for others	(no clear answer)	Not everyone who does it is guilty	1) critical of weak 2) abuse liberty
Participating (immature)	Movie at theater	Has freedom to do it	Yes	No	Convinced but proud	It's not wrong for anybody	Thinks of self as mature	No one who does it is guilty	1) causes weak to stumble 2) license

For Lively Discussion

1. Which of the following statements are biblical and which ones are cultural?

> Christians should not buy a state lottery ticket.
> Christian children should not attend public schools.
> Majority rule is the pattern for decisions in the church.
> A church leader should not drink too much wine.
> Communion bread should not have leaven in it.
> Every Christian should witness to nonbelievers.
> Church board members should rotate every few years.
> Legalism is wrong.

2. Choose an issue mentioned in this first chapter where you know you disagree with other Christians and yet you are convinced it is essential. Use the suggested guidelines to decide whether it is essential.
3. Discuss the definition of a weaker Christian in relationship to spiritual maturity.
4. Why can't we tell whether or not persons are weak or strong on an issue by whether or not they abstain?
5. How is it possible for someone with a very strong opinion on a disputable matter to be a weak Christian on that issue?
6. What may happen if one of the parties thinks of a biblical principle or verse regarding a disputable matter?

CHAPTER NOTES

1. Some Christians appeal to Deuteronomy 22:5 as proof that women should not wear slacks: "A woman must not wear men's clothing, nor a man wear women's clothing, for the Lord your God detests anyone who does this."

   This law may have been designed to prevent practices associated with the cross-sexual garments worn by transvestites or pagan prostitutes in the immoral social and religious culture of ancient Palestine. The robes and other garments worn in biblical times often appear gender neutral (most churches have a visual reminder of this problem when biblical costumes are worn during Christmas or Easter plays).

   If we are going to be consistent in applying this one Old Testament commandment as binding on all forms of dress today, we must also apply other verses in this passage to the same extent such as the instructions regarding bird's eggs (v. 6), mixing seeds (v. 9), mixing wool and linen (v. 11), or the command to wear tassels (v. 12).

Assuming verse 5 is binding for Christians in today's culture, it is difficult to agree on the type of modern clothing which violates the principle without making purely arbitrary decisions. Why is this verse almost always applied to slacks? If this verse applies to Christians in mainstream American culture, what about shirts, belts, shoes, coats, and numerous other styles of clothing that have no gender identification?

Since it is obvious that believers do not keep all the provisions of the Old Testament law (which has been fulfilled in Christ), we must careful not to pick out verses or passages to support our own cultural ideas or traditions. A broader, more serious concern is the practice of using an unclear or highly debated passage as the *sole* support for an absolute position on an issue. This misuse of Scripture most often drives wedges of rejection into otherwise healthy relationships.

2. Religious culture, historical traditions, and even climate dictate styles of clothing. Compare, for example, the Old Order Amish dressed in black, home-tailored clothing, a Scottish Christian man decked out in a kilt, an American Christian in a business suit on Sunday morning, and a native believer in the Amazon River rain forest. Whose clothing style is "right"?

3. Some Christians apply "the lesson from nature" to this issue from Paul's statement: "Does not the very nature of things teach you that if a man has long hair, it is a disgrace to him. . . ?" (1 Cor. 11:14).

    This reference suffers the usual weaknesses of isolated verses in relation to disputable matters. First, this solitary reference to long hair on men occurs as a secondary comment in the discussion of another issue, namely, the headcovering of women. Second, it is not immediately clear what Paul means by "nature." Does he mean nature in the sense of biological nature or natural customs? How would the first view support the need for a woman's headcovering? Third, the lack of a definitive interpretation of that primary issue has led not only to debate on the question of a woman's headcovering, but also to the development of headcovering as a distinctive for some denominational groups. Fourth, any attempt at applying this standard today is left to the very subjective opinion of what constitutes "long" today.

    A biblical "theology of long hair" should also take into

consideration references to the Nazarite vow observed by men like Samson, Absalom's long hair which the Old Testament does not condemn (although it ill-equipped him for fighting!), or the vow observed by four Jerusalem believers in Acts 21. In order to be consistent, some Christians who try to define "long hair" may need to take down most depictions of Jesus!

Most opposition to long hair and beards in the '50s and '60s was based on its association with beatniks and hippies and the culture of drugs and protest. Current hairstyles which often emphasize shorter hair present a totally different difficulty. Short hair or shaven heads follow the styles begun by the "grunge" or alternative music movement and radical "skinhead" groups. Christian men who like closely cut or shaven styles aren't likely to be accused of espousing either of these views.

Both the fact that the definition of the issue shifts when culture changes and that Christians disagree on the specific application of biblical guidelines suggest that this issue of long hair on men is a disputable matter in the area of Christian freedom.

4. I have been unable to shake the effects of an emotionally traumatic event I went through on the issue of dancing while in junior high. I know certain types of dancing may be permissible for some, but as of this writing I am still a weaker brother whose conscience is still not completely free on this issue.

Romans 14:1–12

Accept him whose faith is weak, without passing judgment on disputable matters. One man's faith allows him to eat everything, but another man, whose faith is weak, eats only vegetables. The man who eats everything must not look down on him who does not, and the man who does not eat everything must not condemn the man who does, for God has accepted him. Who are you to judge someone else's servant? To his own master he stands or falls. And he will stand, for the Lord is able to make him stand. One man considers one day more sacred than another; another man considers every day alike. Each one should be fully convinced in his own mind. He who regards one day as special, does so to the Lord. He who eats meat, eats to the Lord, for he gives thanks to God; and he who abstains, does so to the Lord and gives thanks to God. For none of us lives to himself alone and none of us dies to himself alone. If we live, we live to the Lord; and if we die, we die to the Lord. So, whether we live or die, we belong to the Lord. For this very reason, Christ died and returned to life so that he might be the Lord of both the dead and the living. You, then, why do you judge your brother? Or why do you look down on your brother? For we will all stand before God's judgment seat. It is written: "'As surely as I live,' says the Lord, 'every knee will bow before me; every tongue will confess to God.'" So then, each of us will give an account of himself to God.

— 2 —

Whose Side Is God On?

BOB AND CAROL Parker sat down for dinner. The elegant table setting promised a fine meal. They didn't know the Andersens very well, but they did look forward to getting to know them better. Karl and Jean Andersen were godly missionaries who had faithfully served the Lord in Europe for over twenty years.

After Karl thanked God for the food, the dinner began with wine being served. Jean Andersen poured wine into Carol's glass before either Bob or Carol could think. When Jean came to Bob, he politely declined and said, "No thank you. Could I just have water?"

"Sure, Bob," the hostess said.

Jean went on to pour a glass of wine for her husband and herself before returning the bottle to the serving table.

Carol sat awkwardly. She did not want to offend her hostess, but she was very uncomfortable with wine in her glass. Bob sensed her problem and asked, "Jean, would you mind getting Carol some water, too?"

"Oh, I'm sorry," she said. "I'll get you some right away."

Carol was feeling more and more uncomfortable. "I can't believe you people drink this stuff," she blurted. "Do you drink wine regularly? Don't you know that it's wrong for Christians to drink wine or any kind of alcohol?"

Karl Andersen suddenly realized what was happening. "I'm sorry," he said. "We have forgotten our American manners. Please forgive us for serving wine. We are so used to wine in Europe where Christians think nothing about it. We have been drinking wine with our meals for the last twenty years. We always use it in moderation of course."

Graciously, Jean picked up the wine glasses and took them to the kitchen. She came back with water for everyone. Pleasant conversation filled the evening, but Carol still struggled with what had happened. All the way home she vented her strong feelings to Bob.

"Is it really all right for some people to drink wine? How can it be right for Christians in Europe and wrong for us? God doesn't have two standards, does he? Doesn't the Bible teach that it's wrong to drink wine?" The barrage continued. Bob tried to listen and support her feelings, but he had no idea that Carol would do what she did next.

The following day Carol marched into her pastor's office, sat down, and told him what happened. "How long have we been supporting these people?" she demanded. The pastor tried to answer her questions, but it was clear that Carol wanted him to straighten out the Andersens' opinion on alcohol. The pastor assured her he would talk to the Andersens, but Carol was not satisfied.

"What is your opinion, Pastor, should Christians be allowed to drink wine?" Now the pastor felt pinned to the wall. Deftly, he explained the options without giving his personal viewpoint.

Carol left the pastor's office but she was still not satisfied. "Why doesn't the pastor preach on this sometime?" she asked Bob. "How can he allow this type of thing to go on among our missionaries?" Since nothing was said publicly, Carol eventually convinced Bob that they should leave the church.

Our consumer-oriented, feel-good, I-gotta-be-pleased mentality slips into our relationships in the local church. If my church does not meet my needs, I will find a church that does.

Even when disgruntled people stay in the local church, they tend to ignore people in the congregation with whom they disagree. The decisions that have been made in regard to certain issues become fodder for gossip; both ignoring others and gossiping results in broken relationships and disunity.

The church at Rome apparently faced similar dangers in their relationships (Rom. 14:1–12). Radically saved Jews and Gentiles flowed into the church. That was the good news. Unlike most of the major cities in America, these believers in Rome did not have the option of choosing from several good churches—there was only one. These new believers were all incorporated into the same local congregation where they worshipped together and shared their lives with one another in very deep and tangible ways. That was the bad news.

Carol Parker is not the first church member to struggle over this issue; the issue of drinking wine with a meal sprang up among the congregation in Rome. While a person with a Jewish background might have insisted on the observance of the Sabbath and abstinence from nonkosher foods and wine (Rom. 14:21), a Gentile convert probably did not have any difficulty eating ham sandwiches for lunch (Rom. 14:17). The common early church practice of eating meals together undoubtedly presented unique challenges when it came to food and drink.

Practical problem solving did not come soon enough; Jews and Gentiles disagreed on more than one issue and began to avoid one another. Broken relationships deteriorated even more when some of these Christians began to condemn those believers who disagreed with them. The apostle Paul knew what was happening in the church in Rome, and he wrote to the believers out of concern for unity.

In chapter 14 Paul exhorted the members of the church to stop judging each other in areas of neutral issues. Christians today would do well to heed Paul's exhortation because we often slip up on the same issues. For example, I may feel that my personal convictions should be the convictions of others if they want to be pleasing to God. If God is pleased with me and approves of my conviction on a certain disputable matter, then God would be pleased if everyone took my position. Further, I may think that God must not approve of those who do not share my conviction. Since I am convinced that God is pleased with my position, I speak out on the point to tell others what I think God thinks. I tend to make a nonessential an essential—to change a nonmoral matter into a moral question—and then condemn those whom I think are sinning.

When I criticize others, sin has raised its ugly head. The sinner is me—not the one who disagrees with my personal conviction. The sin is my critical spirit toward Christians who do not agree with me—not the wrongness of my conviction. The Lord urges Christians to stop judging each other in these neutral areas for the very good reasons found in Romans 14:1–10. Jesus Christ accepts both opinions as morally right. Jesus Christ is our Lord and Judge, and we are not to take his place in relation to other Christians.

JESUS CHRIST ACCEPTS
DIFFERING CONVICTIONS

Disputable matters always have two sides—the weak and the strong. The weak on a given concern are weak both in faith and in conscience. The weak believe a specific, neutral question is sin.

The strong on a given concern are strong both in faith and in conscience. The strong have specific faith—they believe that they are free to participate without violating their conscience by sinning.

In this context of disputable matters, weak faith is not unacceptable, because God's Word says God has accepted the one whose faith is weak (Rom. 14:3b). God accepts this particular weak faith because he allows differing convictions in areas of neutral issues such as what we eat or drink.

Paul wrote Romans 14:1–10 to speak to both the strong and the weak sides of faith. It is likely that most of the weak in the church in Rome were Christians who had come from Jewish backgrounds where certain foods were forbidden. The strong in the church at Rome were likely the Gentile Christians who felt free to eat and drink anything. Let's reformat the text to highlight those portions that refer to each side.

[Strong:]	**Accept him whose faith is weak, without passing judgment on disputable matters. One man's faith allows him to eat everything, but**
[Weak:]	*another man, whose faith is weak, eats only vegetables.*
[Strong:]	**The man who eats everything must not look down on him who does not,**
[Weak:]	*and the man who does not eat everything must not condemn the man who does, for God has accepted him.*
[All:]	Who are you to judge someone else's servant? To his own master he stands or falls. And he will stand, for the Lord is able to make him stand.

[Weak:]	*One man considers one day more sacred than another;*
[Strong:]	**another man considers every day alike.**
[All:]	Each one should be fully convinced in his own mind.

[Weak:]	*He who regards one day as special, does so to the Lord.*
[Strong:]	**He who eats meat, eats to the Lord, for he gives thanks to God;**
[Weak:]	*and he who abstains, does so to the Lord and gives thanks to God.*
[All:]	For none of us lives to himself alone and none of us dies to himself alone. If we live, we live to the Lord; and if we die, we die to the Lord. So, whether we live or die, we belong to the Lord. For this very reason, Christ died and returned to life so that he might be the Lord of both the dead and the living.

[*Weak:*]   *You, then, why do you judge your brother?*
[Strong:]   **Or why do you look down on your brother?**
[All:]   For we will all stand before God's judgment seat.

Whose side was God on? Both and neither. God accepted both personal convictions, but he rejected as sin the judgmental attitude each side had toward the other. God urges the strong to accept the one who is weak in faith without looking down on the person's personal preference. Thus, if a Christian believed that eating meat was permissible, he or she must not look in disdain at the person who does not eat meat. Neither should the vegetarian critically condemn the Christian who has the freedom to savor a good steak or roast or even ham. Why not? Because "God has accepted him" (Rom. 14:3).

This is a critical principle to remember: God accepts opposite convictions. I might have a deep conviction about some issue while my Christian friend might have an opposite conviction. We both could be right before God! If I condemn my friend's conviction, I have sinned. I may feel that the other individual is sinning, but if I condemn the other person's behavior in relation to some neutral matter—a nonmoral issue—then I am the one guilty before God. It is also possible to be weak in one disputable matter while strong in another. We need to be very careful not to condemn one another in these areas.

JESUS CHRIST IS OUR LORD

Well-meaning Christians sometimes try to point out sin in the lives of others. It is the spiritually mature, though, who are called upon to reprove the clear violation of God's commands (Gal. 6:1–2; 2 Tim. 4:2). Disputable matters are not always clear. When Christians condemn each other in relation to neutral issues, they judge in the Lord's place. God asks in Romans 14:4, "Who are you to judge the servant of another?" Who do we Christians think we are? The Lord? Only the Lord has the right to judge, and in neutral areas, the Lord has already ruled. Both the weak and the strong stand uncondemned.

How can it be possible for God to approve opposite views? One's view on a neutral matter is a personal conviction: "Let each man be fully convinced in his own mind" (Rom. 14:5b NASB). The weak person may be fully convinced that Sunday is a sacred day and that no work should be done. The strong may be equally convinced in his mind that if he works on Sunday, his Lord will not condemn him.

The crucial issue in any disputable topic is personal conviction before the Lord. If one person is able to carve jack-o-lanterns for Halloween and another feels it is wrong, each person may hold opposite opinions and both stand uncondemned before the Lord. If one Christian young man wears longer hair and another feels it is sin, both are approved by the Lord. The Bible says one's practice in neutral areas is a personal matter between the individual and the Lord. Both the weak and the strong do what they do for the Lord and not because of someone else's opinion.

We are to do what we do because we belong to the Lord. We do not live for ourselves but for the Lord. We belong to the Lord, not to someone else in the church. The Lord Jesus Christ lived and died to be our Lord (Rom. 14:9), and as our Lord, he is the ultimate authority in our lives. In disputable matters, he is the only one who should be obeyed. He is Lord of every believer, and no one should take his place by judging another person who disagrees on a disputable matter. Though we can disagree on matters of personal opinion, we cannot condemn the person who disagrees with us on some issue. A critical, condemning attitude is very serious because it is equivalent to telling the Lord to move over so we can take his place in another Christian's life.

Church leaders also must be very hesitant to make any statements or rules that allow leaders to take the Lord's place in regard to another believer's life. Most church leaders do not want to take the Lord's place, but some do it inadvertently.

JESUS CHRIST IS OUR JUDGE

Another reason why the Lord urges us to stop condemning one another is that we may become guilty of taking the Lord's place as Judge. The Bible says: "You, then, why do you judge your brother? Or why do you look down on your brother? For we will all stand before God's judgment seat" (Rom. 14:10). We are not to be one another's judge in the area of nonessentials. Moral issues and sin call for discernment and discipline. Although areas of neutral issues call for discernment, churches should never discipline an individual for personal opinions in these areas.

Unless the Bible gives clear, direct commands regarding an issue, zealous Christians should close the valve that expresses their zeal. Quick condemnation of someone over a debated matter only proves that we think we make a better judge than the Lord does. It also jeopardizes relationships and clouds more important matters.

When we see another believer commit what we believe is a sin, the first question to ask is "Does the Bible speak clearly and directly to this issue so Christians have little debate about its being sinful?" If there is some doubt, refuse to judge. Even if we have no doubt that the issue is a sin, we still need to be slow to condemn and very careful about what we say and do next.

Few Christians would have the audacity to ask an earthly judge to move over in order to take his or her place on the bench. Yet, sometimes our actions and attitudes suggest that we want to take the place of Jesus Christ, our perfect Judge. When we take the Judge's place, both strong and weak Christians tend to condemn brothers or sisters without a trial; but both sides will give an account at the judgment seat of Christ where everyone will be answerable only to the Lord.

Bob and Carol Parker left the church because church leaders did not publicly condemn the Andersens for drinking wine with their meals. The Andersens, as mature missionaries and the strong Christians in this case, should have known in advance that Bob and Carol might be weak Christians whose consciences would not allow them to drink wine. Once they discovered their error, however, they did apologize.

Meanwhile, Carol's attitude went from bad to worse. Her judgmental spirit condemned the Andersens and the pastor. The Bible, however, condemns Carol's attitude as the true sin in this case.

So whose side is God on? He is on the side of the Christian who refuses to condemn someone else who disagrees. The Andersens can keep their conviction, and should be sensitive to any weaker Christians, especially in their American home church. Carol may hold her conviction, too, but she should keep it as her own conviction before God. When she judged the Andersens, she sinned. The Andersens could have slipped into sin, too, if they had passed judgment on Carol's opinion.

We are free to disagree agreeably, discuss the issues, determine the principles, and decide on the wisdom of an action or practice—but we must not condemn the other person. We are to stop judging each other in disputable issues. Why? Jesus Christ, who accepts both positions, is alone our Lord and Judge.

For Lively Discussion
1. In a disputable matter over a neutral issue, whose side is God on?
2. Discuss the difference between the sin of judging and the positive use of judging.

3. Discuss this statement: "If God is pleased with me and approves of my conviction on a certain disputable matter, then God would be pleased if everyone took my position on this issue."
4. How is it possible to be right in the wrong way?
5. What issues have been discussed so far that you think are not "neutral" but wrong for Christians? What attitude should you have toward those Christians who do not share your opinion on this issue?

1 Corinthians 8

Now about food sacrificed to idols: We know that we all possess knowledge. Knowledge puffs up, but love builds up. The man who thinks he knows something does not yet know as he ought to know. But the man who loves God is known by God. So then, about eating food sacrificed to idols: We know that an idol is nothing at all in the world and that there is no God but one. For even if there are so-called gods, whether in heaven or on earth (as indeed there are many "gods" and many "lords"), yet for us there is but one God, the Father, from whom all things came and for whom we live; and there is but one Lord, Jesus Christ, through whom all things came and through whom we live. But not everyone knows this. Some people are still so accustomed to idols that when they eat such food they think of it as having been sacrificed to an idol, and since their conscience is weak, it is defiled. But food does not bring us near to God; we are no worse if we do not eat, and no better if we do. Be careful, however, that the exercise of your freedom does not become a stumbling block to the weak. For if anyone with a weak conscience sees you who have this knowledge eating in an idol's temple, won't he be emboldened to eat what has been sacrificed to idols? So this weak brother, for whom Christ died, is destroyed by your knowledge. When you sin against your brothers in this way and wound their weak conscience, you sin against Christ. Therefore, if what I eat causes my brother to fall into sin, I will never eat meat again, so that I will not cause him to fall.

— 3 —

I Know I'm Free!

"THIS MONEY IS tainted," Phil began. "How can we possibly accept three thousand dollars for a new gymnasium from people who don't even know the Lord?"

Frustration oozed from Stan's tone, "Why do we care about that when we borrowed from a bank full of unbelievers?"

"We do have to consider the motives of the Culver family," Howard offered in his usual wise thinking. "Perhaps they think giving to our church impresses God enough to let them into heaven. We certainly wouldn't want to encourage that idea."

"Suppose they have no ulterior motives." Stan continued. "What prevents us from accepting this money?"

Phil wasn't convinced. "I would still like to know why they are doing it."

As the debate continued, Stan became more and more discouraged. With finality he said, "There is no passage of Scripture that tells us that this money is somehow tainted. I believe we are free to take it and use it." He hoped his remark would settle the matter.

"The Bible doesn't address a lot of issues directly," Phil countered. "But I believe we have biblical principles to apply in this situation."

"Like what?" Stan wondered.

"Like not selling the gospel," Phil responded. "Like not allowing our church to be run by unbelievers."

After much more discussion, the church board decided not to take the money. They lovingly explained their position to the Culvers and used the occasion to talk with them about their relationship with Jesus Christ.

In the first century, thrifty church members saved money by purchasing marked-down meat in the market. Some church people later discovered that the meat was marked down because it had been used in the ritual worship of pagan deities in the city. Now what? Reaction was split. Some Christians refused to buy it. Others had no problem with the bargain meat.

Meat used in ritual worship was apparently divided three ways: one part was burned on the altar; another part was given to the pagan priest; and the third part was given to the one who brought it as an offering and who believed that the gods enjoyed the aroma of the burning meat. Leftovers not used by the priest were then marked down and sold at a substantial discount in the local market where it could be purchased by the people. The one who had brought the offering might also have served a portion to Christian friends at a dinner party.

The urgent questions were: Should Christians buy the marked-down meat? Should they serve it to guests? The believers in the city of Corinth disagreed.

Both sides probably claimed verses to support their positions. Some said, "No, this is meat offered to idols," convinced that it would be a sin to eat such meat anywhere, anytime. They doubtless pointed to the early church's wisdom principles found in the letter sent to all the churches in Acts 15:29: "You are to abstain from food sacrificed to idols, from blood, from the meat of strangled animals and from sexual immorality. You will do well to avoid these things."

Others likely said: "It's all right to buy this marked-down meat because food does not defile." They could have appealed to the Lord's question in Mark 7:18–19, "Are you so dull? . . . Don't you see that nothing that enters a man from the outside can make him 'unclean'? For it doesn't go into his heart but into his stomach, and then out of his body. (In saying this, Jesus declared all foods 'clean')." Therefore, some Corinthian Christians felt at liberty to buy the marked-down meat because it did not bother their strong consciences.

Usually, Christians hold convictions based on their understanding of the Bible. When Phil and Stan debated whether to accept the Culvers' money, Phil based his convictions on certain biblical principles that he felt were pertinent to the issue. Stan, by contrast, was equally convinced that the Bible did not forbid one's receiving money from non-Christians. The disagreement over how principles from Scripture relate to a neutral issue is what makes the issue debatable.

In Corinth, the strong were so convinced of their position that they asked Paul about it when they wrote to him (see 1 Cor. 8:1). Perhaps they said, "Anyone who knows anything about idols knows they are nothing. Idols cannot affect the meat, and eating the meat offered to idols cannot affect us. Why can't these fellow members in our church understand their freedom in Christ? What do you say, Paul?" Paul responded by writing about their knowledge of freedom in Christ in this one area of neutral things in 1 Corinthians 8. What Paul said to them provides principles for application to any area of Christian liberty.

KNOWLEDGE OF FREEDOM IS
ENTIRELY INSUFFICIENT

Most Christians understand that an idol has no power, but not everyone exercises this knowledge in practical living (1 Cor. 8:7). The strong believer's intellectual decision led to prideful insensitivity toward the weaker members of the church. Knowledge divorced from love inflates the mind and feeds conceit. Knowledge puffs up; love builds up. J. B. Phillips translates 1 Corinthians 8:1b as: "While knowledge may make a man look big or act like a know-it-all, love builds into people beautiful qualities of Christian character."

Is anything wrong with a ten-dollar bill? Could something happen to money if it passes through the hands of an unbeliever? How about pumpkins? Should I not be free to eat pumpkin pie made from a jack-o-lantern after the Halloween party? Some Christians insist that no activity, however satanic it might have been, can do anything to corrupt any object. Carving a jack-o-lantern cannot corrupt the pumpkin or somehow taint delicious pumpkin pie. We should all recognize that an inanimate object cannot be morally corrupted even if it can be somehow accompanied by evil spirits.

Knowledge, however, is not enough of a guide for dealing with neutral issues. If I insist on carving a jack-o-lantern because I think it is fun, and I have no sensitivity to my Christian friend who does not have the freedom to join me, then my knowledge lacks love and operates at a deficit. Knowledge of my freedom is entirely insufficient to govern my actions in the body of Christ. Those who think knowledge is enough do not know as much as they need to know. Those who think they know do not know. To know I am free in the Lord to enjoy so-called marked-down meat is not enough. I must also realize my responsibility to express love.

KNOWLEDGE OF FREEDOM IS
THEORETICALLY CORRECT

The truth is that "there is no such thing as an idol in the world" (1 Cor. 8:4). Our world has many "graven images" carved out of wood or cast in bronze, gold, and other materials. None of these images has any power, so they exist and have power only to the degree that the worshipper conceives them to have such. There is only one self-existent God. Any other "god" is an impostor and exists only because a mortal imagined such a deity.

Someone may ask, "But aren't there many gods that people worship?" We find the answer paraphrased from 1 Corinthians 8:5–6: "Maybe for them, but not for us. There may be many gods, but for us there is one God—our Father, the Source of all things, and we are created for his glory. There may be many lords, but for us—one Lord, Jesus Christ, Mediator of all in creation, our Mediator in our new creation."

Indeed, the second commandment—a prohibition against idols (Exod. 20:4–6)—has been violated continuously. What an infinitely poor substitute an idol is! No created deity, graven image, or idol does anything. An idol has no ability to change the condition of the meat offered to it; thus, the marked-down meat in the marketplace could not corrupt the Corinthians.

In our day a pumpkin carved to make a jack-o-lantern or money used by satanic worshippers cannot hurt you or your ministry. Neither is a picture of Jesus on the wall a "graven image." Paint, brush strokes, and a frame do not have moral significance, nor does the resultant product itself have moral value.

How an "image" is used may violate the clear commands of Scripture, so cautious judgment should be used. So the strong Christian may have the right answer on the Bible trivia exam, but theoretical knowledge falls woefully short in helping to resolve differences in the church today just as it did in the church at Corinth. Such knowledge may actually make things worse if the knowledge is applied without love.

KNOWLEDGE OF FREEDOM ALONE IS
POTENTIALLY HARMFUL

Some in Corinth had the knowledge, faith, and strength of conscience to eat the marked-down meat. In a similar way, some Christians today feel free to observe Halloween with a harvest party, carved jack-o-lanterns, and gory pranks.[1] As Christians, we must consider not only the intrinsic nature of a neutral issue but also the subjective state of mind of the person participating.

The weak Christians in Corinth felt it was sin to eat meat sacrificed to idols. Because of their upbringing, earlier habits, or former lifestyle, the weak still believed that they were participating in idol worship by eating the meat. The Bible suggests that some in Corinth could not shake their past. Listen to the way Paul explains it: "Some people are still so accustomed to idols that when they eat such food they think of it as having been sacrificed to an idol, and since their conscience is weak, it is defiled" (1 Cor. 8:7).

A weaker brother can have strong convictions *and* a weak conscience. A very strong-willed Christian with very definite opinions may not feel free to participate in certain neutral matters. The weak tend to "judge him who eats" (Rom. 14:3 NASB), which is the problem. They feel so strongly about their personal conviction that they leave the impression that the opposite position is morally wrong simply through their tone of voice. The weak and the strong are each to "be fully convinced in his own mind" (Rom. 14:5b). Some Christians may have a strong will, strong emotions, and a weak conscience. Weak Christians become easily agitated or even defensive because of the strong emotions they feel.

The word *accustomed* (1 Cor. 8:7) highlights one of the key reasons for the heated debate on neutral things such as buying and eating marked-down meat. Every person has woven into them living patterns, habits, and belief systems that make up their emotional fiber. Sometimes a traumatic event can "burn" a person emotionally. The personal convictions that the person feels in his or her core being is covered with emotional scars. He or she remains emotionally tender if the same issue resurfaces later.

For example, after a drug addict turns to Christ and is radically transformed by Christ's power, a flood of emotions returns when events remind him or her of their past darkness. Or, if a child was severely disciplined for going to a movie theater, his or her emotional conviction may run deep and strong against going to movies. If a Christian family's belief system communicated that all dancing was morally wrong, then the child when he or she becomes an adult is likely to find it difficult to emotionally embrace that which the mind has come to believe is permissible. Although these persons may be technically defined as weak in conscience, they nevertheless have strong convictions.

Christians today who have difficulty accepting the fact of their freedom in Christ often cannot shake the guilty feelings they have because of some past emotional trauma in relation to an issue. A traumatic past experience may prevent them from developing the emotional strength that they need to break free from a deeply held conviction. True head knowledge may not be enough to enable a Christian to shake free from a developed conviction.

Some Christians in Corinth also struggled with the emotions of their past. Since they were accustomed to thinking of the marked-down meat as associated with idol worship, they did not feel free to eat it. Their conscience condemned them (1 Cor. 8:7b). If they had tried to ignore their consciences and had listened to others tell them that eating the meat was permissible, they would have been in danger of committing sin against their consciences.

I can have the head knowledge that I am free and still have my conscience doubting whether I should go ahead and participate. In such a case my knowledge is insufficient and even potentially harmful. I must pay attention to the personal inner conviction prompted by my conscience because God's Word says, "The man who has doubts is condemned if he eats, because his eating is not from faith; and everything that does not come from faith is sin" (Rom. 14:23). When in doubt, don't.

Most Christians today realize that eating or not eating marked-down meat will not affect us one way or the other. Nor will our decision improve our spiritual life one way or the other (see 1 Cor. 8:8). Such knowledge, however, could do spiritual damage, however. Our liberty might trip up a weaker brother or sister spiritually.

After teaching these principles in a church in Portland, Oregon, a godly woman came up to me after the session to make me more aware of the dangers facing Christians in Portland. She told me that she ministers to the Mien people from Vietnam who have moved into houses surrounding the campus of Multnomah Bible College and Biblical Seminary. She found that family members who had become Christians did not know what to do at meal times because the food was prepared, first offered to family idols, and then served to the family. These new believers were asking her whether they should eat the meat which was offered to idols. We went over these principles again to provide loving wisdom for these Mien Christians.

It was important to understand the doubt of these people and respect their consciences. We decided that these Mien Christians could be advised to go ahead and eat the family's food since the idols would not alter the food itself. But since some of them might not feel free to do so right away, their consciences would need to be respected. The Bible says, "Be careful, however, that the exercise of your freedom does not become a stumbling block to the weak" (1 Cor. 8:9).

What's the danger? The danger is this: if I exercise my freedom in the presence of another Christian whose weak conscience will not allow participation, then my actions may tempt the weaker brother to think he would not sin if he does participate. If he does participate, however, he violates his own conscience. "If someone sees you, who have knowledge, dining in an idol's temple, will not his conscience, if he is weak, be strengthened to eat things sacrificed to idols?" (1 Cor. 8:10 NASB).

It is important to remember that in Romans 14–15 and 1 Corinthians 8–10 weaker believers are not defined by the likelihood of their choosing to violate their consciences. Some weaker Christians may be more susceptible than hard-headed, determined people who would never think of violating their consciences. But even hard-headed, determined people would still consider it sin if they ever did violate their consciences. Weaker Christians are defined by their opinion in relation to the issue, not by whether they might ever succumb.

Paul's concern, however, is the danger facing the susceptible weaker brother who might violate his own conscience when he sees the stronger person participating. The Bible places the burden on the strong. When the strong flaunt their freedom without regard for a fellow Christian who disagrees, "he who is weak in ruined, the brother for whose sake Christ died" (1 Cor. 8:11 NASB). If you act on the basis of knowledge that you are free in Christ to participate and have no thought or care for a nearby Christian whose convictions differ from yours, "you sin against Christ" (1 Cor. 8:12b). The sin is not in exercising your liberty but in exercising your liberty at the expense of fellow believers. The conclusion? If somebody else might be hurt spiritually, the strong Christian should give up the freedom to participate. The highest principle governing my choices in disputable matters is love for a fellow believer who might disagree with me on that issue.

A key point to remember is this: a mature awareness of my freedom in Christ allows me to lovingly give up my personal rights for the sake of my fellow Christian.

Did the church board do the right thing in refusing the money from the Culvers? If the Culvers thought their gift would impress God enough to let them into heaven and the church board accepted the money with knowledge of their motives, the board would be operating with knowledge but without love. Suppose, however, that the Culvers had no expectations from God or the church. Perhaps in such a case the money could be accepted.

Whether the Culvers had ulterior motives or not, the money itself could not corrupt anyone. The key element in the board's decision was Phil's struggle to believe that the Lord would approve their actions if they accepted the money. Phil may have represented others in the congregation who felt it would be wrong to take the money. The board made a wise choice out of deference to those who felt it was wrong. How a church makes a decision on neutral issues calls for a whole chapter by itself (see chapter 12).

What about Halloween? Do some believe carving jack-o-lanterns somehow exposes people to the power of the demonic? Should the church allow the youth group to have a Halloween party? Again, if some feel it is wrong, church leaders need to be sensitive to those members of the body who have a personal conviction that such things should not be done by Christians.

I have a responsibility to think about my brothers and sisters in Christ. I cannot participate in my freedom and not care who knows it. I may know that I am free, but mature knowledge loves others supremely. I give up my freedom in a loving way for the sake of others in my church.

Giving up my freedoms sounds like I live a boring, joyless life—I may never enjoy my liberties in Christ because somebody might be hurt. Paul's teaching requires that I defer to those who may be close by or to those who may see my actions and be hurt by them. If I deferred to all Christians everywhere, I probably would not even get out of bed in the morning! On every doubtful issue, there is a weak Christian somewhere who believes my actions or ideas are sinful. It is unlikely that they all attend my church or are in my circle of acquaintances. My responsibility is to love those nearby who disagree with me and to respect the consciences of other Christians with whom I come in contact.

For Lively Discussion

1. Which of the following objects are inherently morally wrong?

_____ A cigar
_____ A jack-o-lantern
_____ A ouija board
_____ A picture of Jesus
_____ An R-rated film
_____ A switchblade

2. Which issue has stirred up your emotions most to say it must be wrong for Christians?

    When and how did this issue develop as a conviction for you?

    Can you describe a life experience which caused you conflict on this issue?

3. Whose responsibility is it to give in (or defer) to the other when Christians disagree on a neutral issue?

4. How can a weaker Christian become strong in relation to a certain issue?

5. Should a weaker Christian keep from announcing weakness if this Christian is also a teacher, leader, or pastor?

CHAPTER NOTES

1. The principles governing wisdom regarding the dangers associated with occultic elements will be discussed more fully in chapter 7.

Romans 14:13–23

Therefore let us stop passing judgment on one another. Instead, make up your mind not to put any stumbling block or obstacle in your brother's way. As one who is in the Lord Jesus, I am fully convinced that no food is unclean in itself. But if anyone regards something as unclean, then for him it is unclean. If your brother is distressed because of what you eat, you are no longer acting in love. Do not by your eating destroy your brother for whom Christ died. Do not allow what you consider good to be spoken of as evil. For the kingdom of God is not a matter of eating and drinking, but of righteousness, peace and joy in the Holy Spirit, because anyone who serves Christ in this way is pleasing to God and approved by men. Let us therefore make every effort to do what leads to peace and to mutual edification. Do not destroy the work of God for the sake of food. All food is clean, but it is wrong for a man to eat anything that causes someone else to stumble. It is better not to eat meat or drink wine or to do anything else that will cause your brother to fall. So whatever you believe about these things keep between yourself and God. Blessed is the man who does not condemn himself by what he approves. But the man who has doubts is condemned if he eats, because his eating is not from faith; and everything that does not come from faith is sin.

— *4* —

Love-Limited Liberty

SIRENS PIERCED THE evening air. Tires screeched around corners as a police car chased the blue Chevy down the city street. The suspect sideswiped a parked car, ran a stop sign, ran over someone on a bicycle, and topped out at seventy miles per hour in a thirty-five miles-per-hour speed zone. At a roadblock the driver pulled out a gun, shot and killed a police officer, and sped on, continuing to break dozens of laws. On straight stretches of road, his speed reached ninety miles an hour, but he failed to negotiate one sharp curve. The blue Chevy smashed into a concrete wall. At that moment, the suspect was removed from the jurisdiction of all the human laws he had broken. He was dead.

Death ends the jurisdiction of the law. What was true of the speeding suspect in relation to man's laws is true of every believer in Jesus Christ. Because of our identification with the death of Jesus Christ, we have been set free from the jurisdiction of God's own law and its condemnation. "There is therefore now no condemnation for those who are in Christ Jesus. For the law of the Spirit of life in Christ Jesus has set you free from the law of sin and of death" (Rom. 8:1–2 NASB).

Our death with Jesus Christ releases us from the need to try to measure up to the law's demands. We had to die to the law and be joined to Christ to be able to live the Christian life because our own efforts to keep God's law could never be successful. Only the Spirit of God in us produces what pleases God.

Christians sometimes struggle when the Bible says not to

grumble, lust, judge others, or be a money-grubber. The Bible's demands are tough, and most Christians want to obey. Some try hard, only to fail again. Does the difficulty of keeping God's laws as a good Christian mean that I must continue to feel defeat and guilt? Do I just keep struggling to do better? That is not what the Bible says. The Bible teaches that I am free from the law that stirs up my struggle with sin (see Rom. 7:4–6; Gal. 5:1).

So why do I keep feeling defeated? God's law is doing its job. The purpose of God's law is to keep me on my knees! The very fact that I feel defeated proves that God's commands are doing their job. My need to obey God's commandments drives me to completely depend on the indwelling Spirit. The Christian life is an impossible life apart from daily dependence on Christ. When God's Word tells me not to complain, to be thankful in everything, or to be patient, I must go to my knees. I pray in faith believing that he will transform me. Then, I get up off my knees, get going, and trust him.

Christ died to set us free from the principle of law-keeping. Well-meaning Christians often try to put other believers back under law to please God. God is not pleased, because the Bible says, "It was for freedom that Christ set us free" (Gal. 5:1). Because we are free, we do not have to listen to anyone who wants to force us into trying to keep any kind of law for salvation or for sanctification. We are free from the law, and we are free from the demands of well-intentioned but legalistic people who insist that we should live the Christian life according to certain rules and expectations. Each Christian is free to live by his or her own conscience before God in areas of neutral things. We are free to enjoy everything God has created.

As Americans, we value freedom, and the freedom we value follows rules. In much the same way, a train is free to roll but only if it stays on the tracks. Liberty, therefore, is not license. True freedom conforms to a standard. It is not coerced. Someone has recommended to Americans that the Statue of Liberty on the East Coast be supplemented by a Statue of Responsibility on the West Coast. Such a balance would be a helpful reminder. We need to recognize the same balance in our Christian life. Rights bring responsibility. Although Christians have been set free from the law, another law limits our liberty in Christ—the law of love. We balance our freedom from a list of do's and don'ts with our love for others.

"Great! I'm free!" Rufus said. "I'm glad the Lord set us free because ham is one of my favorite meats, but Jacob told me I shouldn't eat it if I wanted to be a good Christian. Now I can enjoy eating it without worrying about Jacob and his hangups about pork!"

"Hold on," Paul responded. "I believe you can enjoy ham, too, but you have to consider Jacob's feelings about this."

Jason looked puzzled. "But I thought you just said we're free."

"We are," said Paul. "We are free to love Jacob and do what's best for him, but sometimes we have to limit our liberty."

Rufus was getting discouraged. "Why should we?" he asked.

The apostle Paul's response to this fictitious dialogue is recorded in Romans 14:13–23. In this portion of Scripture, we find at least three major reasons to limit our liberty: to avoid causing a brother to sin, to avoid degrading our freedom in Christ, and to pursue mutual encouragement.

TO AVOID CAUSING A BROTHER TO SIN

"I don't want to cause problems for Jacob," Rufus said, "but I still don't understand. I thought Jesus declared all foods clean and told Peter to eat ham and a lot of other foods considered unclean."

"That's true," Paul went on. "I know and am convinced in the Lord Jesus that nothing is unclean in itself, but to him who thinks anything to be unclean, to him it is unclean."

"So you agree with me!" Rufus said, feeling encouraged.

"Yes," said Paul, "It's true. My personal conviction permits me to eat ham. I not only know in my mind that this is what Jesus taught, but I am also fully persuaded in my heart."

"Let's go tell Jacob. Maybe he'll change his mind." Rufus said hopefully.

"But it's not that simple. He may still feel in his heart it would be wrong."

"Are you saying that even though eating ham is not a sin, I must not eat ham when I'm with Jacob because he considers it a sin?" Rufus tried to understand, but he was struggling with the possibility that he would have to limit the occasions when he could enjoy ham.

"You're basically correct," Paul said. "If you ignore Jacob's conviction because you like ham, you're hurting him not loving him."

The strong must decide not to trip up the weak spiritually (Rom. 14:13). When Rufus eats with Jacob, Rufus should avoid ham since Jacob's conscience will not let him eat ham, having been raised to be a good Jew and told never to eat nonkosher food. Rufus must recognize the potential spiritual danger for Jacob. If Rufus insists on eating ham in Jacob's presence, Jacob could be tempted to eat it, too, which would make Jacob sin against his own conscience.

Perhaps Jacob does not know about his freedom. If what he lacks is knowledge, then Rufus can tell him, and Jacob might immediately be free to participate. It's more than likely, however, that even after Jacob knows he can enjoy ham, he will still struggle with the emotions of his upbringing. Only the Holy Spirit brings to the heart and conscience full liberty of faith in any neutral area.

Although the apostle sided with the strong in his personal convictions, he acknowledged the convictions of the weak. The conscience of the weak is entitled to respect. The inability of the weak to be free from a condemning conscience is not a moral defect, nor is the conscience going to be automatically released through head knowledge. A spiritually mature person who is weak in a certain neutral area may need much time to work through deeply felt emotions before the conscience is freed.

Liberty exercised without love hurts others in the church. Liberty exercised without regard for Christ's love destroys another person's spiritual health. Food, or any other neutral issue, is not worth it when it hurts someone else.

TO AVOID DEGRADING OUR
FREEDOM IN CHRIST

Jason, who had been silently following the conversation, finally jumped in. "So, if he eats a ham sandwich when he's with Jacob, Rufus may cause a confrontation with Jacob?" Jason was beginning to see the point.

"Why make a ham sandwich the issue?" continued Paul. "For the kingdom of God is not a matter of eating and drinking, but of righteousness, peace and joy in the Holy Spirit."

Another reason to limit the exercise of our freedoms is to guard against remarks that condemn our liberty. Paul says, "Do not allow what you consider good to be spoken of as evil" (Rom. 14:16). The strong only invite verbal condemnation from the weak when they flaunt their freedoms. When Paul sided with the strong on an issue, he may have expected to hear some words of disagreement from several weaker brothers. Why allow other people to drag down and condemn something we enjoy? If we limit our freedoms, we avoid unnecessary disapproval.

When tangible, physical issues like whether or not to eat a ham sandwich replace spiritual concerns like righteousness, peace, and joy, our priorities become warped. Many things that we choose to "take a stand on" are not worth the trouble they cause because they merely major on the minor. Neutral issues such as ham sandwiches cannot be the standard that we use to determine our association with other believers. Often the issues that split churches are physical, philosophical, methodological, or personal. Some Christians launch a crusade in support of a very flimsy viewpoint. Strong opinions do not automatically transform a nonessential into a fundamental of the faith. Christians who fling verbal barbs at one another only damage the church.

So what issues are non-negotiable upon which we must stand firm? Some issues are clearly essential such as the deity of Christ, the inspiration of the Bible, or salvation by faith rather than works. Each person must decide on a list of essentials based on the criteria mentioned in chapter 1. For me, the most decisive criteria for deciding upon a disputed issue is "Would I die for my conviction?" Is it an essential issue for the universal body of Christ? Would I tell a firing squad "Go ahead and shoot me" for my opinion on a disputable matter? Not me!

We must limit our liberty in order to stay focused on the main issues. Love-limited behavior serves Christ, is acceptable to God, and is approved by men. Although we need not take the position of the weaker brother on an issue in order to be pleasing to God, we do need to defer to the weaker brother in order to be acceptable to God as a servant of Christ.

TO PURSUE MUTUAL ENCOURAGEMENT

"My relationship with Jacob is more important than ham sandwiches, right?" Rufus concluded with a little hesitancy.

"Right," Paul said. "Do not destroy the work of God for the sake of food. No food or drink issues should split the body of Christ. Jesus declared all foods clean, but it is wrong for a man to eat anything that causes someone else to stumble."

"It's not fair," Rufus grumbled. "I have to give up eating ham sandwiches when Jacob and I eat together, and he doesn't have to give up anything."

"The responsibility rests on the strong to defer to the weak," Paul said. "It is better not to eat meat or drink wine or to do anything else that will cause your brother to fall."

Too many strong-headed Christians stir up trouble because they believe that they alone are right. Even if they are right on a particular topic, it may be the wrong one. What issues should they pursue?

Paul said, "Let us pursue the things which make for peace and the building up of one another" (Rom. 14:19 NASB). Some cantankerous church members hunt for opportunities to disagree or dissent simply for the joy of the hunt and the kill. Shooting fellow soldiers to prove a point only puts holes in the church's line of defense against the Enemy of our souls. The Bible exhorts us to search for ways to avoid the eruption of unhealthy conflict in our churches. Jesus blessed peacemakers not troublemakers (Matt. 5:9). Whenever Christians disagree with each other, somebody should ask whether the disagreement is important enough to give up the pursuit of peace.

Not all conflict reflects carnality. The Bible encourages us to "examine everything carefully; hold fast to that which is good" (1 Thess. 5:21 NASB). Healthy concern and sincere, loving questions may be the prompting of the Holy Spirit to guide church members toward needed change.

Jealousy, selfish ambition, arrogance, and personal agendas fuel fiery words that destroy otherwise healthy relationships (James 3:6, 14). When a healthy church debate degenerates into bitter anger, unkind words, and broken relationships, then God's people are sinning. Some church members never fully recover. Others move to different locations and continue to smolder, ready to ignite new disasters.

What we should be doing is dousing the flames. We need churches full of people whose passion is peace. When words are sown in peace, churches grow. James says: "Peacemakers who sow in peace raise a harvest of righteousness" (James 3:18).

Peacemaking is the job of every Christian, but the Lord holds the strong responsible for deference to the weak. Paul says, "It is better not to eat meat or drink wine . . ." (Rom. 14:21). The Bible mentions drinking wine more than once. The church in America is filled with weak members in regard to drinking any alcohol. Danger lurks for Christians who come from alcoholic backgrounds, and our society is rightly angry at those who drive drunk.

Whether the wine of the New Testament was fermented or not, the church today is fragmented over this issue. Disagreement is like a red flag, marking the question as a potential neutral issue. Paul waved his red flag— not over grape juice (drinking fruit juice isn't a problem for anyone) but over drinking wine. The problem in Rome remains a problem in America. Christians disagree. Paul's advice? Limit your liberty out of love for brothers and sisters who hold a different conviction. A person who exercises love-limited liberty refuses to be associated with alcohol.

Our guiding principle should be to build each other up rather than tear each other down.

BIBLICAL GUIDELINES FOR NEUTRAL THINGS

Paul concludes his discussion in Romans 14 with three crucial guidelines for Christians in the area of neutral issues.

The first guideline is "The faith which you have, have as your own conviction before God" (Rom. 14:22a NASB). In the context of decisions about neutral issues, faith is very important in relation to a specific disputable matter. The Bible instructs each Christian to have a standard of behavior in relation to each issue. You are encouraged to have a personal conviction, but your conviction should be held with the awareness that you answer to God.

The New International Version's translation of the first part of verse 22, "whatever you believe about these things," is fine. It continues the verse, however, with a translation that suggests that no one else should know what our conviction might be: "Whatever you believe about these things keep between yourself and God." The point, however, is not that we should never let our convictions be known to anyone. The point is that we should not make our personal conviction everyone else's standard for behavior. The strong person's conviction will be the exact opposite of the conclusion of the weak Christian on the same concern. We must know one another's positions in order to avoid causing someone to stumble.

A second guideline is "Happy is he who does not condemn himself in what he approves" (Rom. 14:22b NASB). Christians who mentally convince themselves to take part in some disputable matter will not be happy if their consciences condemn the action. If you approve of certain actions, make sure you are honest with yourself. Siding with the strong at the expense of inner peace is a sad thing. If you truly do not feel condemned, you may enjoy your freedom before the Lord.

A third guideline is "But the man who has doubts is condemned if he eats, because his eating is not from faith; and everything that does not come from faith is sin" (Rom. 14:23). When a neutral issue registers in your mind and heart as a doubtful issue, you would be sinning if you participated. Knowledge is not enough. You must be able to act from the heart, not just the head. When in doubt, don't.

If you are looking for a standard to use to decide whether or not a gray issue or a disputable matter is wrong for you, ask yourself whether you have the faith to believe that you could do it in God's presence and not sin.

Your conclusion about what is right and wrong in relation to a disputable matter will be different from other Christians. The Lord allows alternative views in the neutral realm. God permits two people to hold opposite convictions. However, God does hold you responsible for what you believe is right or wrong for you. If you have faith to believe an issue is not sin for you, then be sensitive to others who differ. You have a responsibility to limit your freedom for their sake.

For Lively Discussion
1. Read Romans 7:1–6, Galatians 2:16–17, 20–22, and Galatians 3:2–5. Discuss the Christian's relationship to the commands of the Bible.
2. What are the three reasons to lovingly limit our liberties?
3. What can a strong Christian do to help a weak Christian become strong?
4. What are some ways we can obey this command: "Do not allow what you consider good to be spoken of as evil"?
5. Discuss how this statement relates to decisions about neutral things: "Everything that does not come from faith is sin."
6. In what situations would it be possible for a strong Christian to become weak?

Romans 15:1–13

We who are strong ought to bear with the failings of the weak and not to please ourselves. Each of us should please his neighbor for his good, to build him up. For even Christ did not please himself but, as it is written: "The insults of those who insult you have fallen on me." For everything that was written in the past was written to teach us, so that through endurance and the encouragement of the Scriptures we might have hope. May the God who gives endurance and encouragement give you a spirit of unity among yourselves as you follow Christ Jesus, so that with one heart and mouth you may glorify the God and Father of our Lord Jesus Christ. Accept one another, then, just as Christ accepted you, in order to bring praise to God. For I tell you that Christ has become a servant of the Jews on behalf of God's truth, to confirm the promises made to the patriarchs so that the Gentiles may glorify God for his mercy, as it is written: "Therefore I will praise you among the Gentiles; I will sing hymns to your name." Again, it says, "Rejoice, O Gentiles, with his people." And again, "Praise the Lord, all you Gentiles, and sing praises to him, all you peoples." And again, Isaiah says, "The Root of Jesse will spring up, one who will arise to rule over the nations; the Gentiles will hope in him." May the God of hope fill you with all joy and peace as you trust in him, so that you may overflow with hope by the power of the Holy Spirit.

— *5* —

How to Disagree Agreeably

"WHAT DO YOU enjoy doing that you know some Christians feel is wrong?" Greg, the small-group leader, asked.

"I really enjoy watching a good movie on the big screen in a newer theater with stereo sound systems surrounding me," said Dave.

"You mean like *The Dream Is Alive* at the Omnimax Theater?"

"That's really special," agreed Dave. "But I enjoy movies like *Aladdin* or *The Lion King*, or a classic like *Fiddler on the Roof.*"

"OK, would you be willing to give up going to such movies for the sake of someone else in the church?"

"Is there really someone here who thinks one of these movies is wrong?" Dave wondered aloud as he looked around the room.

"Let's say there is another couple who would be genuinely hurt if you went."

"If they would be hurt, sure. But I would find out who it is and avoid the subject around them." Dave felt good about his solution.

"One of the easiest ways to build relationships is by having fun together. Women may play tennis or shop. Men may golf or hunt. Families can camp together. Couples can enjoy a barbecue and a good movie afterward," the leader continued. "What if you meet a couple in the church who believes it is wrong to go to movies? Would you invite them to your barbecue? Probably not. It's easier to relax with people we agree with. When was the last time you did something with someone you didn't know well? Too many times we run with the same bunch. It's comfortable. It's tough to relax in new relationships, especially if you find that you disagree on leisure activities."

Christians do disagree. Sometimes we enjoy an interchange of opinions, and we give our reasons for our opinions. We might hope to change someone's mind. The interchange of ideas, wisdom, and biblical principles could stimulate healthy discussion and guide decisions. The difficulty is to keep the discussion stimulating without being destructive because when we become angry or frustrated, we border on sin. Conversations that become destructive leave bitterness in a relationship. Then, if we decide to avoid each other completely, we violate the commands of Scripture.

Churches need members who are trained in the skill of healthy disagreement. Skill in disagreeing would help us all live in harmony. As we have seen, the Bible gives the freedom to individuals to disagree and for both to be right. In first-century Rome the hot issues were the observance of certain days as holy, abstinence from eating meat, and the drinking of wine. Today those issues are still debated, and many more could be added to the list. How can Christians today avoid making lists when what is freedom for one is felt to be sinful by another?

Is my conviction more important than my relationships? If the issues are clear in the Bible and foundational to my faith, probably so. If my opinion on an issue is not something I would die for, then what? Who is right? Who gives in, since Scripture teaches that both sides in a dispute could be right at the same time on the very same issue?

God is more concerned about our attitude toward one another than he is about our opinion on an issue. It is possible to be right in the wrong way. Therefore, in areas where the Bible gives freedom to disagree, we have the responsibility to disagree agreeably. Romans 15:1–13 gives two ways to disagree agreeably. Each of the two imperative verbs in this passage gives one key to skillful disagreement on neutral issues. The first command is "each of us should please his neighbor for his good" (Rom. 15:2a), and the second is "accept one another" (Rom. 15:7a).

PLEASE ONE ANOTHER

The first command places the responsibility on the strong believer (Rom. 15:1–6). The strong must please the weak. "Each of us should please his neighbor for his good, to build him up" (Rom. 15:2). To please someone in this context of neutral things means to behave in ways that build up the weak spiritually. Just for a moment, think of a debated behavior on which you are strong. Now ask yourself, "Am I willing to give it up?"

Suppose your mother-in-law thinks that all dancing is wrong, and you want your daughter to take ballet lessons. Who gives in? If your mother-in-law has a legalistic, pharisaical attitude about all types of dancing, you might choose to ignore her opinion. Jesus sometimes ignored the Pharisees. In Mark 2:23–28 Jesus' disciples picked heads of grain to eat as they passed through the grain fields on the Sabbath day. Jesus knew the traditional convictions held by the Pharisees, yet he said nothing to his disciples to warn them or to stop them from offending the Pharisees. Sometimes Jesus went ahead in spite of the legalistic traditions and opinions of Pharisees. In Mark 3:1–6, Jesus knew the Pharisees were watching to see if he would heal a man who had a withered hand on the Sabbath. He looked at the Pharisees in anger for their lack of compassion and healed the withered hand anyway. Jesus chose his battles carefully.

To return to the difficult, hypothetical situation with the mother-in-law's opinion about dancing—you might need to decide whether or not this is the topic on which to risk her legalistic condemnation. Notice that the command of Romans 15:2 is to *please our neighbor*. Our neighbor is not necessarily the one next door but may be the Christian who is close by. Our behavior depends on who is nearby. If your mother-in-law lives in a different state, you might be able to let your kids learn ballet. On the other hand, if you have frequent contact, you might need to defer.

Is this situational ethics? No. Neutral issues have no inherent moral or ethical value in and of themselves. Yes, our decisions on these nonmoral matters depend on the situation. Our action depends on who is nearby.

George rolled down the road to the music of his favorite country-and-western radio station. He passed a stranded motorist whom he recognized as Rick, a fellow believer from his church. George pulled off the road, got out of the car, and walked toward Rick.

"Can I help?" George asked.

"Am I glad to see you!" Rick sighed. "It just died."

"I can take you to the next service station or a car-repair place if you would like," said George.

"Thanks! I'd sure appreciate it."

As George headed back toward his car, he remembered that Rick was offended by country-western music, a result of playing guitar for several years in a honky-tonk band prior to accepting Christ. George faced a decision. The moment he sat in the driver's seat he would have to make a decision. He could either start the car and the country-western music would come on; he could reach over and turn the radio dial to another station; or he could turn off the radio. Because George wanted to do what was best for Rick's spiritual life, George reached over and turned off the radio. Then he started the car.

When George turned off the radio, he obeyed the Bible's command to please his neighbor in relation to neutral issues like country-western music. George gave up his right to listen to music he enjoyed to avoid hurting his relationship with Rick.

What if George had learned about Rick's personal conviction after Rick climbed in the car and heard the music? George would still be responsible to turn off the country-western music to avoid offending Rick and to avoid a possible argument. If Rick had begun to criticize country-western music, perhaps a gentle apology would have been enough on George's part. If Rick had insisted on labeling country-western music as sinful, George might politely disagree. In any situation, the goal is always to pursue peace in the relationship.

George did the right thing by turning off the country-western music, but we might wonder whether George wanted to do what was best for Rick or whether he was more concerned about what Rick might think of him. The first motive comes from love for Rick, whereas the second motive arises out of fear of Rick's criticism. If George was afraid that Rick's criticism would degrade his enjoyment of country-western music, then the Bible allows for either motive or both. The Bible says: "Do not allow what you consider good to be spoken of as evil" (Rom. 14:16).

Rick met the qualification of someone who was close by. Let's raise another question in relation to the concept of deferring to Christians who are close by. What happens if "my neighbor" is someone who lives in my house? Ralph held the opinion that his wife could wear tastefully tailored slacks to church services, but his wife, Jane, did not feel that women should. Who submits— Ralph or Jane? The Bible puts the responsibility on Ralph to defer to his wife in order to please her. Ralph's wife should be allowed to disagree with her husband, and Ralph should not be upset if she wears only dresses to church.

Let us turn the situation around. What if Jane thought that it was all right to wear slacks and Ralph thought she should not? Then Jane needs to defer and do what would build up her husband. She should wear dresses, not because it is her personal opinion, but because she needs to please her husband who is weak on this issue.

How far do we take this? How much freedom should we give up for the sake of someone else in the body of Christ? The Bible calls attention to Jesus Christ, our example, who gave up his freedoms for our sake. "For even Christ did not please himself" (Rom. 15:3a). If Christ did not please himself, we should follow his response in relation to one another. Christ's example was predicted by Scripture, and Scripture provides what we need when we give up what we enjoy for the sake of a relationship. "For everything that was written in the past was written to teach us, so that through endurance and the encouragement of the Scriptures we might have hope" (Rom. 15:4).

When I give up my freedoms, I need endurance. How long must I give up my freedoms? I limit my liberty as long as a weaker Christian is close by. This is tough to do if I am married to one! What keeps me going? The Bible's encouragement. When I give up my liberties on neutral issues, I am doing what is right. I should not give up hope. I can be fully assured that God is pleased when I seek to please someone close by in order to build them up spiritually.

"Lord, help me!" may be what we feel like crying when we think about giving up a cherished freedom for someone else's sake. Sometimes the strong Christian feels as if the full weight of responsibility bears down upon him or her. The apostle Paul anticipated the Christian's cry and wrote a prayer in Romans 15:5–6. He starts his prayer by saying, "May the God who gives endurance and encouragement give you a spirit of unity among yourselves as you follow Christ Jesus" (Rom. 15:5). Perseverance to keep giving up what we enjoy comes to the person who turns to God who gives endurance. Paul prays for unity among Christ's followers who disagree in these areas. We do not all need to have the same opinion to have harmony.

ACCEPT ONE ANOTHER

The Bible's command to "accept one another" (Rom. 15:7–13) provides the second key to being able to disagree agreeably. Allowing disagreement may be a huge step in the right direction for an opinionated Christian, but mere tolerance can be cold.

Agreeing to disagree cannot be the final goal if the negative attitudes continue to cause huge barriers in the relationship. Therefore, we often need an attitude check so we can disagree agreeably. Acceptance requires love. To accept one another means we extend our sincere, pure love—a warm hug, a handshake, a smile, or an invitation to the next get-together. An action that shows love is necessary, even if the love is hard to feel.

Disagreement sometimes leads to angry words and hurt feelings. When that happens, forgiveness and a readiness to admit sinful attitudes become keys to restoration so that we can enjoy one another even though we still disagree. Although we hurt, we are to show love by our actions. In Rome, former Jews had to get along with Gentiles in the same congregation. Paul expected Christians from diverse backgrounds to welcome one another with open arms. Again, the Lord Jesus provides the example for us to follow. Just as Jesus Christ accepted both Jew (Rom. 15:8) and Gentile (Rom. 15:9–12), so we should accept one another. The apostle Paul cites many Scriptures to prove God's acceptance of Gentiles.

No doubt the Jews found it most difficult to accept Gentiles in the church in Rome. The struggle depicted in the book of Acts confirms the uneasiness that Christian Jews felt when they had to receive former Gentile "dogs" into the assembly as fellow members of one body. Christians from fastidious Jewish backgrounds may have shuddered to watch Gentile converts enjoy ham and wine. How could the Lord possibly approve of such behavior?

Some Christians today give the appearance of being from the Gentile-dog camp to those who have a long history of exposure to the traditional ways of Bible-believing "Jews." Some of these Gentiles feel free to smoke or chew tobacco, dance, or to have a picture of Jesus on the wall. These former heathens might carve jack-o-lanterns or drink wine with their meals. How could Jesus possibly approve? Yet, "God has accepted him" (Rom. 14:3b NASB). The scrupulous Christian "Jew" must learn to accept the "Gentile" and vice versa. Why? Because "Christ also accepted us" (Rom. 15:7). The apostle Paul anticipated that "Torah-thumping" Jews would want scriptural proof that the Lord God accepts Gentiles. So, Paul quoted 2 Samuel, Psalms, and Isaiah to amass evidence of God's plan to accept Gentiles (Rom. 15:9–12).

The Bible does not want doubtful matters to be a barrier, and neither should we. The Christian does not have to agree that something is permissible or right, but he or she is commanded to maintain an attitude of acceptance and unity toward any Christian who holds the opposite opinion on a matter.

Those Christians who feel free to work on Sundays, to dance, and to join Easter-egg hunts must put out the welcome mat to the weak believers nearby. To disagree agreeably means to give up freedoms for the sake of others in the congregation. Why? Jesus Christ accepted them just the way they are. He did not make them change their opinions. The burden of responsibility is on the strong to give up doing those things that another Christian feels is wrong. The need to accept one another, based on the pattern provided by our Lord Jesus Christ, prompted Paul to write another prayer in Romans 15:13 to parallel verse 6. Paul wrote, "May the God of hope fill you with all joy and peace as you trust in him, so that you may overflow with hope by the power of the Holy Spirit."

We sometimes find it difficult to hear the Bible tell us to give up things we enjoy for someone else's sake. We wonder how long we have to limit our liberties in certain relationships. Will our weaker friends ever become strong? Will we ever be able to enjoy our freedoms? We need this prayer in Romans 15:13. We need to know that we are doing the right thing, and we need to know a God who will give us joy and peace as we give up our liberties. We will abound in hope only by the power of the indwelling Spirit as we sacrifice for the sake of people whom God loves.

Christians who do disagree often fight over minor issues. Their disputes may cause them to feel tensions in their relationships until they do not enjoy being with each other. How do they resolve their disputes? The most common way out is to separate. Disgruntled Christians sometimes form another church across town. From a safe distance each embattled group sends verbal missiles of hate toward one another, or each group puts a cold lid of tolerance over a volcanic inferno of bitterness. The church's legacy of wrecked and battered lives stands as a sober monument to Satan's victorious battles.

In many American cities and towns, a new church is not what is needed since we already have a "cafeteria" of churches from which to choose. American consumerism teaches us to choose another church when we become upset with the first. Avoidance becomes a way of life rather than an occasional style of conflict management even if we stay in the same local assembly. We avoid these people— at least on certain subjects. Our human tendency is to avoid; God's way is to accept. When we handle disagreements over neutral issues our way rather than God's way, we are really failing to disagree agreeably.

"What about your relationships?" Greg asked. "Have you protected yourself or have you reached out to those who disagree with you?" Greg looked back toward Dave. "If you knew that a certain couple in this church thinks that going to movies is wrong, would you invite them to your barbecue if it meant giving up a good movie afterward?"

Dave thought a moment. "Sure. I'd invite them over, give them a warm welcome to my home, and choose another way to have some fun together."

Greg smiled. "Thanks, Dave. I'd love to come to your next barbecue."

"You're the one?!"

"Yes. Suzanne and I have yet to feel free to go to movies although we realize we may be the only ones in the whole congregation. I hope no one in this class thinks less of us. We certainly don't want to cut off relationships."

"Don't worry," Dave said. "We have really come to appreciate your teaching. It would be easy to put out a welcome mat to you and Suzanne."

"I'm glad," the leader said. "But it's not always so easy. Many other hot debates could divide several of us in this group. The Lord Jesus prayed for unity among us, and we need the skill to disagree agreeably. How do we do it?"

"We look for ways to please one another," said Dave, "and we welcome each other even though we disagree." Dave continued, "A barbecue is a great idea! Everyone is invited to our place this Friday night."

For Lively Discussion

1. Do you think there is ever a time when a mature, knowledgeable weak Christian should go ahead and participate for the sake of an immature strong Christian?

2. Think of something you enjoy doing that you know some Christians probably feel is wrong. Would you be willing to give this up in order to build a relationship with the one who thinks it is wrong?

3. How is it possible for a Christian to have the right opinion or viewpoint on a given issue and still be wrong?

4. If we have a disagreement with another Christian, what attitudes or actions, according to Romans 15:1–13, should govern our relationship with that person?

5. In relation to neutral things, if you act one way around one

person and another way around another person, why isn't your action hypocritical?

6. Have you been continuing to reach out in love to those who disagree with you? Think of at least one person who should be closer to you but your disagreement has made the relationship awkward. Write down (or think up) one simple yet creative way to "reach out" to that person this week.

1 Corinthians 9:19–23

Though I am free and belong to no man, I make myself a slave to everyone, to win as many as possible. To the Jews I became like a Jew, to win the Jews. To those under the law I became like one under the law (though I myself am not under the law), so as to win those under the law. To those not having the law I became like one not having the law (though I am not free from God's law but am under Christ's law), so as to win those not having the law. To the weak I became weak, to win the weak. I have become all things to all men so that by all possible means I might save some. I do all this for the sake of the gospel, that I may share in its blessings.

— *6* —

Freedom to Win the Lost

TWO MEN MET at a church convention. To their surprise, they discovered that both of them had been blind and that Jesus had opened their eyes so they could see.

One said, "Isn't it wonderful the way Jesus makes mud and puts it on your eyes and tells you to go and wash? When you go and wash, your eyes are opened!"

"Mud?" the other questioned. "Jesus doesn't need to make mud. He just speaks the word, and immediately blind eyes are opened, and you can see."

"Oh no," insisted the first man. "Jesus uses mud."

"No, he doesn't. He didn't use mud on me."

The argument continued to heat up until one said, "If he didn't use mud to open your eyes, then I can't fellowship with you because you're denying one of my essential convictions." He left the convention angry, determined to broadcast his conviction. Soon he had a little group gathered together in his home. They were men and women whose blind eyes had been opened by Jesus' use of mud. They excluded all others and called themselves Mudites.

Meanwhile, another group formed across town. They were people whose eyes had been opened when Jesus simply spoke a word. They encouraged others who had been healed this way to join their group, and they called themselves Antimudites.

For the rest of their lives these two groups continued their rivalry while all around them, groping in darkness, were people who did not know that Jesus had come to give light to them.

Ridiculous? Not really. This parable captures recent church history, which is strewn with the litter of divisions, splits, and denominational provincialism. Meanwhile, the light of Christ's love barely flickers in many communities, and the lost stumble and fall. Instead of reaching out to the lost, Christians would rather debate other Christians within the "safety zone" of the church where the underlying rule is "love one another" than talk to an unbeliever whose fundamental attitude toward Christians is often one of ridicule and rejection.

As Christians grow in the faith, they find it more difficult to relate to their former lifestyle, culture, and friendships within a pagan culture that is now repulsive to them. For many churchgoers, witnessing to the unbeliever in this country has become a major cross-cultural experience. We do not know how to act. We feel that we have so little in common, and we do not want to be put into an awkward situation. These feelings will not go away, but neither will our God-given responsibility to share the good news of God's love for a lost world.

CROSS-CULTURAL COMMISSION

We sometimes forget why the Lord left his church on the earth. He commanded the church to be a witness to the lost. Jesus said, "But you will receive power when the Holy Spirit comes on you; and you will be my witnesses in Jerusalem, and in all Judea and Samaria, and to the ends of the earth" (Acts 1:8). He promised us the power to overcome our fears in order to do the job that he left us on earth to do. Christians have no option if we want to be obedient. We must penetrate our unsaved culture with the gospel message. Jesus said: "Therefore go and make disciples of all nations, baptizing them in the name of the Father and of the Son and of the Holy Spirit, and teaching them to obey everything I have commanded you. And surely I am with you always, to the very end of the age" (Matt. 28:19–20).

With this message Jesus addressed our fears. We have the promise of his personal, indwelling presence. We do not have to venture out to our work associates and neighbors alone. We can trust him to provide wise bridge-building words to reach the unsaved. The task is clear— we are on this earth for one basic purpose and that is to win the lost. The only reason for leaving us as ambassadors in a sin-sick, dark world of people alienated from Christ is to proclaim the message of reconciliation. To reach across cultures may take some adjustment, but by doing so we are being obedient. According to 1 Corinthians 9:19–23, Paul modified his behavior when around the lost in order to win some. Notice how many times Paul restates the goal:

> Though I am free and belong to no man, I make myself a slave to everyone, to *win* as many as possible. To the Jews I became like a Jew, to *win* the Jews. To those under the law I became like one under the law (though I myself am not under the law), so as to *win* those under the law. To those not having the law I became like one not having the law (though I am not free from God's law but am under Christ's law), so as to *win* those not having the law (emphasis mine).

If we focus on our disagreements with one another in the body of Christ, we dissipate our effectiveness in reaching the lost. Non-Christians in America watch as Christians verbally bloody one another, and they wonder why they should join the fight.

CULTURAL COMPLEXITIES

No culture in the modern world has been so strongly influenced for so many years by biblical Christianity than the United States of America, where 86.5 percent of the population claims Christianity as their religion and evangelicals constitute 43.7 percent of the total population.[1] In the South and Southeastern United States, society reflects the impact that Christian values have made. Aberration from certain traditional Christian norms has been unacceptable (although in the tobacco-growing South, deacons still light up a cigarette on the church steps). As recently as the mid-1980s in one public junior high school in an upscale neighborhood in Alabama, students could be expelled if they had dice, cards, or any gambling paraphernalia in their lockers.

Christianity's influence has reached the highest office in the United States. Four recent American presidents sought to capitalize on the power of the evangelical movement in America. President Jimmy Carter unabashedly associated with his Baptist home church in Georgia. Ronald Reagan captured many of the Christian Right's votes during his two terms in office by appealing to Christian moral issues. President Bush was nominally Christian, and President Bill Clinton's religious roots apparently tap into the southern Christian mind-set as well. The word *Christian* is politically acceptable though Christian precepts are not.

On a nonpolitical level, however, many nonbelievers in America think of Christians as people with very strict standards in neutral areas. Pharisaical Christians trumpeted many of these standards so loudly for so many years that non-Christians equate Christianity with a no-fun lifestyle. It is almost impossible to find a Christian depicted in the movies or on television who is mentally, emotionally, and socially balanced. Religious persons are habitually characterized as narrow-minded fanatics or dangerously deranged persons on the fringes of society. The secular American image of Christians includes people who hold pro-life signs on the curbs of America, or John 3:3 signs at a nationally televised football game.

The "don't-dance, don't-drink, don't-smoke" message of Christians, once heard in the context of a predominantly Christian culture, is now heard within the non-Christian society. Christians were once thought of not only as people who did not have any fun but also as people out of touch with their culture. Christians and non-Christians have now reversed some of their roles and each has adopted parts of the other's lifestyle. A more health-conscious society now advocates the "don't drink, don't smoke" message to young people while Christians gather by the thousands at Christian rock concerts.

The complexity of American culture intertwined with Christianity as well as the bombardment of mixed images of what it means to be a Christian should awaken evangelicals to the need to give a clearer message of the Christian faith. More than ever, Christians need to clarify the separation between the essentials of the gospel message and the nonessentials plastered over Christianity in a complex, quasi-Christian culture. Faith in the person and work of Jesus Christ must not be obscured by some arbitrary requirement like getting a haircut or throwing out rock music. If the Holy Spirit makes the seeker aware of some area of sin and the seeker brings it up, we can reassure that person by telling about the Lord's strength to do what is right once he or she has placed trust in Jesus Christ as personal Savior.

Equally complex are the nonessential standards that unbelievers have for Christians, which may be stricter than Christians themselves have. Believers, who have strength of faith and conscience to believe that they can occasionally smoke a pipe or cigar, need to realize that non-Christians may expect Christians to be non-smokers. Christians who are free to dance might have an unsaved neighbor who has always thought that Christians do not dance. The complexities of our culture sometimes make Christians "project the expected image" in order to reach the lost. Other occasions may require the careful dismantling of the image before someone can see what it really means to be a Christian.

CULTURAL CHAMELEON CHRISTIANS

Although the word *chameleon* is almost always used in a negative sense, there is a sense in which it represents a positive approach to for Christian witness. The chameleon is known for its ability to adapt and change color depending on the color of its surroundings. In the same way, Christians who are most effective in their Christian witness have an ability to adapt to the cultural situation. Chameleon Christians have three major assets: they are strong; they are wise; they are balanced.

Chameleon witnesses are strong Christians.[2] Paul said: "Though *I am free and belong to no man*, I make myself a slave to everyone, to win as many as possible" (1 Cor. 9:19, emphasis mine). Let us face it—the strong Christian makes a better evangelist. The strong Christian is free to adapt to any social condition for the gospel's sake. Paul put it this way. *"I have become all things to all men so that by all possible means I might save some.* I do all this for the sake of the gospel, that I may share in its blessings" (1 Cor. 9:22b–23, emphasis mine). The apostle Paul's evangelistic strategy was designed so that he could *become* all things to all men so that by all possible means he might save some.

The apostle did not compromise the gospel, nor did he ever rationalize sinful behavior. He did, however, give up certain rights and freedoms in order to reach scrupulous Jews. He could, for example, observe certain old covenant regulations without compromising the gospel. He could respect the observance of certain festivals and days or refrain from certain nonkosher foods if it meant that he might be able to reach somebody with the gospel.

When Timothy joined Paul in preaching the gospel, Paul had him circumcised because all the Jews in the area of Lystra and Iconium were aware that Timothy's father was an uncircumcised Greek. Paul was aware that Timothy's background might be a barrier in reaching Jews (Acts 16:1–3), so Timothy gave up his right to remain uncircumcised. Although Paul vehemently rejected circumcision as necessary for salvation or sanctification, he required it for Timothy. Why? Paul knew that whatever was not important to the gospel could be changed so that the gospel would not be hindered. Circumcision was one of those things. Paul refused to circumcise Titus for the same reason so the gospel would not be hindered in Paul's attempt to reach the Gentiles (Gal. 2:3).

When Paul sought to reach the Gentiles who were not under the Mosaic Law, he felt free to enjoy pork. He did not try to please religious people or live according to the standards of his Jewish upbringing when he was witnessing to Gentiles.

Christian liberty allows every believer to be a Spirit-directed chameleon who changes behavior around unbelievers in order to evangelize them. Paul said it this way:

> *I became like a Jew*, to win the Jews. To those under the law *I became like one under the law* (though I myself am not under the law), so as to win those under the law. To those not having the law *I became like one not having the law* (though I am not free from God's law but am under Christ's law), so as to win those not having the law (1 Cor. 9:20–21, emphasis mine).

Paul became like the ones he was trying to reach with the gospel so that nonessentials would not be a barrier.

Like Paul, we are free to win the lost in any Christ-honoring way that we can. Christians must not confuse holy living with personal opinions and the traditions of Christian culture. Someone who refuses to go to the ballet is not more holy than a Christian who goes. A Christian who would never take his lunch break with fellow employees whose pagan life-style is embarrassing has bound himself or herself by personal rules that prevent healthy interaction. Christians who are free from stifling rules and legalism can make better evangelists.

What if I am a weak Christian on some controversial issue? Does that mean I should not witness until I have knowledge and freedom of conscience to participate? Christians with doubts about an activity should not participate in it even if it might jeopardize their reaching the lost. The Lord does not ask us to sin to reach the lost. We are commanded to witness but not at the expense of our personal convictions. What we can do is allow those who are strong the freedom to go ahead with whatever activity may be doubtful for us personally. If we are weak and get caught in an awkward situation, God will provide wise words so that we can creatively avoid personal sin without making the nonessential behavior a barrier to communicating the essential Christian message. Becky Pippert relates her experience with such a situation in her book *Out of the Saltshaker and Into the World.*

> A girl moved below me in my apartment building in Portland, Oregon. Every time I saw her she was on her way to another party. We always exchanged friendly words and one day she said, "Becky, I like you. You're all right. Let's get together next week and smoke a joint, okay?"
>
> I replied, "Gee, thanks! I really like you too, and I'd love to spend time with you. Actually I can't stand the stuff, but I'd sure love to do something else."

Of course she looked a bit surprised, not so much because I didn't smoke grass, but because I had expressed delight at the thought of spending time with her. I could have told her, "I'm a Christian and I never touch the stuff," but I wanted to affirm whatever I possibly could without selling short Christian standards. Too often we broadcast what we "don't do" when we should be trying to discover genuine points of contact. Most of us tend either to over-identify and blend in so well that no one can tell we are Christians or to separate ourselves and play it safe by having little contact with the world. We should recognize what our tendency is and work against it.[3]

Chameleon witnesses are wise. The best evangelists are not only free but also wise. God's people need wisdom in order to discern the standards of each person or cultural group and adapt accordingly. One of the most important questions we should ask of anyone we hope to reach with the gospel is "How would you recognize someone who is a Christian from someone who is not?"

Sometimes the response is "Christians don't swear, smoke, or dance; they go to church and never enter a tavern." Wisdom pays attention to this response. To reach this person with the gospel means the Christian must check for any sinful habits and make some minor adjustments to his or her lifestyle. Suppose, for example, Mike is a Christian man who occasionally loses his temper and uses profanity. In order to win the unsaved person, he needs to trust the Lord for victory in this area of his life and surrender his unruly tongue to the Lord. Mike doesn't go into taverns, so that part of the Christian image isn't hard to maintain. Since the person he is trying to reach is his neighbor, he will want to be very regular (and maybe visible) as he leaves Sunday morning to attend church. Let us say that the really tough one is to give up square dancing classes. If sacrificing this one form of personal entertainment will win an unsaved person to Christ, then he must. Maybe we do not witness more because we find it hard to live up to the high expectations some non-Christians have for us!

Sometimes the response comes from a belligerent person who says, "Christians are phonies and hypocrites." In this case I do not want to live up to his expectations! No follower of Jesus Christ is free to be a hypocrite. The Bible leaves no room for disagreement on this issue. The wise evangelist makes an effort to communicate integrity and honesty so that this person will see a Christian who is not a phony.

The intricacy and complexity of building effective relational bridges to reach the lost calls for huge doses of instant wisdom. Most conversations will not wait until we can fine tune our words. We simply have to look to the Lord to guard our tongues. Colossians

4:5–6 says to those of us in the church, "Be wise in the way you act toward outsiders; make the most of every opportunity. Let your conversation be always full of grace, seasoned with salt, so that you may know how to answer everyone."

Christians need wisdom to discern the culture, but they also need to make wise decisions for their own moral safety, or the moral safety of others close by. Exercising our liberty in order to reach countercultural lifestyles requires moral discernment and common sense. Talking to an attractive, aggressive member of the opposite sex alone in a home may not be sinful, but many Christians would be advised to be like Joseph and run away from temptation. Certain questionable areas of Christian liberty remain unwise choices for witnessing Christians. Simply because my lost neighbors enjoy a certain activity does not mean that I must exercise my freedom and also participate. If participation means moral danger for me, then wisdom finds a way not to participate without forcing my neighbor into thinking that nonparticipation is essential to being a Christian.

Believers who want to have an impact on worldly cultures face a tough barrier—the fear of condemnation by other Christians. We want to be accepted by others in the body of Christ. The risk of feeling disapproval or outright rejection can effectively kill our motivation to reach the lost. To complicate matters further, some disparaging remarks may come from fellow believers who, because they are susceptible to a particular activity, may be caused to stumble spiritually by our freedom. More often, however, the critical comments come from people with pharisaical attitudes who are zealous to maintain an appearance of self-made purity.

The strong must defer to genuinely weaker Christians in order to protect them. For example, children in the home are taught strict standards of behavior for their own moral safety. If an activity would not be healthy for the kids, perhaps the strong Christian should defer (see chapter 9).

What if complaints about your witnessing come from legalists in the church? The Lord rarely deferred to the demands and laws of the Pharisees. He chose his battles. Christians who are trying to reach the lost by occasionally exercising freedom in a questionable area will have to be willing to take the criticism in order to accomplish the higher goal. How do we know who is a genuine weaker Christian and who is being legalistic or pharisaical? We do not always know for sure. The chameleon Christian will have to exercise wisdom and listen for clues about what fellow Christians believe regarding a disputable matter.

Chameleon witnesses are balanced. The Christian chameleon in any culture changes behavior without sliding into isolation on the one hand or immersion on the other. A radical identification with the culture to the point of losing your distinctive Christian message must always be balanced against a radical rejection of the culture to the point of losing your contact with unsaved people.

We must ask ourselves four questions to discern a wise balance between the sin of becoming just like the lost world and the self-centeredness of cutting off any impact we have as ambassadors in this world.

Is this a neutral issue?

Am I weak or strong on this debated matter?

Would my refusal to participate truly jeopardize the gospel?

Would my participation for the sake of evangelism actually cause my genuinely weaker brothers and sisters in Christ to stumble?

Most of the time, wisdom dictates the development of a creative alternative to participation in a disputable matter. However, if only Christians who are being legalistic complain, it may be worth the battle. Our commission to witness for Christ is clear, but we need the wisdom that only the Lord can provide to carry it out.

For Lively Discussion

1. What happens to my ability to witness if I am a weak Christian on some neutral thing?
2. Discuss this statement: "Many nonbelievers in America think of Christians as people with very strict standards on neutral issues."
3. What is the balance between immersion in the world and isolation from the world?
4. If you invited several of your unsaved neighbors over for a barbecue, and one of them offers to bring beer, how would you respond?

CHAPTER NOTES

1. Statistics from Patrick Johnstone, *Operation World: The Day-by-Day Guide to Praying for the World* (Grand Rapids: Zondervan, 1993), 563–64.
2 . I am indebted to the work of Dr. Joseph Aldrich in his book *Lifestyle Evangelism* (Portland: Multnomah Press, 1981), chapters 2 and 3, for many of the concepts found in this chapter.
3. Rebecca Pippert, *Out of the Saltshaker and Into the World* (Downers Grove: InterVarsity, 1976), 120–21.

1 Corinthians 10:12–22

So, if you think you are standing firm, be careful that you don't fall! No temptation has seized you except what is common to man. And God is faithful; he will not let you be tempted beyond what you can bear. But when you are tempted, he will also provide a way out so that you can stand up under it. Therefore, my dear friends, flee from idolatry. I speak to sensible people; judge for yourselves what I say. Is not the cup of thanksgiving for which we give thanks a participation in the blood of Christ? And is not the bread that we break a participation in the body of Christ? Because there is one loaf, we, who are many, are one body, for we all partake of the one loaf. Consider the people of Israel: Do not those who eat the sacrifices participate in the altar? Do I mean then that a sacrifice offered to an idol is anything, or that an idol is anything? No, but the sacrifices of pagans are offered to demons, not to God, and I do not want you to be participants with demons. You cannot drink the cup of the Lord and the cup of demons too; you cannot have a part in both the Lord's table and the table of demons. Are we trying to arouse the Lord's jealousy? Are we stronger than he?

— 7 —

Wisdom in Participation

THE OREGON COAST provides spectacular vistas high above the pounding surf. Several locations allow convenient places for one to park, get out, and move toward the fence at the edge of the cliff. Clear weather brings rewarding views of the Pacific, especially when the whales are migrating.

These locations are so exhilarating that people sometimes get the urge to jump (with the mistaken delusion that they can fly). Others decide to ignore the warnings and venture across the safety fence to get a better look or to feel a rush of excitement that comes with defying the odds. They walk right up to the edge and challenge danger and death.

Have these daredevil cliff walkers done something wrong? Unless a governmental regulation or law is broken, these cliff walkers have not committed a crime. Walking on the extreme edge of a cliff when there is no prohibition cannot be labeled as sin.

Are the daredevils wise? Most reasonable people would agree that unnecessarily choosing to flirt with danger or even death is not the smartest decision one can make.

Like the daredevil cliff walkers by the Pacific, some Christians insist that they can walk on the edge of a moral cliff with no difficulty at all. Perhaps some can. The rest watch in fear. The Bible appeals to us to make wise decisions, and Christians disagree on what is wise. In nebulous neutral issues, Christians sometimes argue over where to place the safety fence.

The application of wisdom in neutral issues relates to the problem of temptation. Temptation is not sin. Neither is a tempting thought. A tempting thought becomes a sinful thought when we stop the thought, talk to it, and invite it in to stay for awhile. Thus,

85

we should actively identify tempting thoughts. Sometimes we are oblivious to what we are thinking, and this passivity opens the doors to all kinds of damaging thoughts.

One way to "grab" our thoughts is to engage in what is referred to as healthy self-talk. Once we are aware of a tempting thought, we can cleanse our minds by reciting an appropriate Scripture, praying (aloud if possible) for enabling grace to get God's perspective on the sin, reiterating God's opinion about the sin, thanking God for the victory in advance, and then turning our thoughts to "whatever is true, whatever is noble, whatever is right, whatever is pure, whatever is lovely, and whatever is admirable" (Phil. 4:8).

Temptations come in different forms for different folks. A dangerous temptation for one person may not be the same for another. A Christian delivered from the stranglehold of alcohol probably faces greater danger in a tavern or bar than one who has never had the problem. A former addict needs to place the safety fence much further away from the danger zone than do other Christians. The "cliff principle" holds true even when each Christian has a different location for the safety fence. Although liberty can be exhilarating, wisdom refuses to hop over the safety fence to walk in a danger zone. Neutral issues have cliffs and danger zones; they require safety fences.

THE NEUTRAL SCALE

Areas of Christian liberty fall on a continuum. However, not all neutral concerns are equal. Some questionable areas of behavior would not be wise, while others may be very permissible.

The following line chart, "The Neutral Issues Scale," can be helpful in thinking through debatable issues. If I chose to eat chocolate ice cream, very few people in my culture would consider my action sinful. Most people would classify my choice as very permissible (from my perspective, even preferable!). On the other end of the spectrum, however, if a person chooses to drink alcohol, many people in our society would object—especially fellow church members. While consuming alcohol isn't a crime (unless one is underage), drunken driving is a chronic social problem and the focus of much stricter laws. The daily consumption of alcoholic beverages would certainly put that person and others at risk in a number of ways. This issue would have to be classified further toward the morally wrong end of the scale.

The Neutral Issues Scale
Application of Wisdom

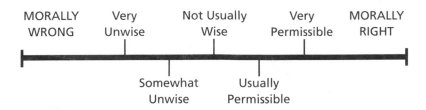

| MORALLY WRONG | Very Unwise | Not Usually Wise | Very Permissible | MORALLY RIGHT |

Somewhat Unwise   Usually Permissible

Let's combine the cliff principle with the Neutral Issues Scale. Each person must decide where to put the safety fence for a given issue. A Christian who is weak on a certain issue will need to put the fence further back from the "morally wrong" end of the scale because any participation would be morally wrong for the one who is weak in faith and conscience. Although some may not be sinning when they engage in a particular action, the one who has doubts is condemned if he tries it (Rom. 14:23).

Christians who disagree on the wisdom of a certain activity must realize that what is wise for one person may be unwise for another person. Real wisdom allows for differences in the application of wisdom in each person's life. On the one hand, the believer who is weak should apply wisdom in setting behavioral boundaries both for themselves and for their relationship to the strong members of the local assembly. On the other hand, the strong Christian limits his or her liberty by common sense and wisdom in relation to neutral things, especially for the sake of reaching unbelievers with the gospel.

Christians must learn to apply wisdom to obtain a healthy balance between isolation and immersion in relation to the lifestyle of people outside of the body of Christ. As mentioned earlier, the one who has strong faith to believe that neutral issues are not wrong makes the best soulwinner. However, the strong believer should watch for the danger of walking too close to the moral edge.

So, what if an unsaved co-worker invites me to have a drink after work? What if he invites me to a nightclub or a heavy-metal rock concert? Should I go? If I have to question whether I should go, I probably should not.

A similar question was raised by the Christians in Corinth. The parties at the local hangouts were fun, and they had enjoyed the festivals in the past (after all, anything with costumes, ram's horns, a band, and a leg of lamb sounds exciting!). Besides, these

Christians did not want to offend their old friends. Some Christians in Corinth said, "Why not?"

Paul responded by saying, "Watch out!" To illustrate the danger, Paul reminded the Corinthians of various privileges that Israel had possessed and how they had fallen into sin anyway (see 1 Cor. 10:1–11). Then Paul warned the daredevil cliff walkers: "So, if you think you are standing firm, be careful that you don't fall!" (1 Cor. 10:12). Walking on the edge may not be sin for the strong in faith, but usually such behavior is not wise. Some situations put temptations before the believer that are too hard to resist. Resisting temptation requires wisdom. A favorite verse of many occurs in a context that urges those with strong faith to apply wisdom in areas of Christian liberty. Paul said: "No temptation has seized you except what is common to man. And God is faithful; he will not let you be tempted beyond what you can bear. But when you are tempted, he will also provide a way out so that you can stand up under it" (1 Cor. 10:13).

What is Paul's advice here and what was the wise way out for the Corinthians? Paul's counsel to the Corinthian church seems clear: "Therefore, my dear friends, flee from idolatry. I speak to sensible people ["I speak as to wise men" in the NASB]; judge for yourselves what I say" (1 Cor. 10:14–15). Paul recognized that the issue did not involve a moral absolute but rather the application of wisdom because going to a party in Corinth and eating food offered to idols were not sinful actions.

THE APPEAL TO THE WISE

The order to flee from idolatry reflects a wisdom based on God's command for us not to worship other gods or graven images. Idolatry in Corinth involved the worship of pagan deities. Idolatry is clearly sin and occurs when a person expresses belief in the supreme worth of someone or something other than God himself. When something or someone has become an idol in our lives, it has become more important than God. When we want something so badly that we will sacrifice the things of God in order to have it, then that something has become an idol. Americans sometimes consider material possessions, recreation, or even family relationships as more important than God. Idolatry is one of the deeds of the flesh according to Galatians 5:20.

What does God want us to do with apparently harmless activities associated with idolatry? The parties and festivals associated with those gods became the questionable activity. Paul's appeal is for us to flee from sin and to flee from everything that might lead into sin. Avoid anything that is questionable as well as anything that borders on sin.

The patriarch Joseph provides a good model. When Joseph found himself alone in the house with the boss's attractive and sexually aggressive wife, he immediately sensed the danger. When she grabbed him by the robe and asked him to sleep with her, Joseph left his robe in her grasp and ran out of the house. Joseph did not want to linger at the edge of the morally wrong cliff. The temptation was too great.

Immediately preceding the discussion of neutral issues in Romans 14–15, Paul said, "Put on the Lord Jesus Christ, and make no provision for the flesh in regard to its lusts" (Rom. 13:14 NASB). The Bible commands us to flee from sin and to make no room in our lives the wants of the sinful nature. In other words, move the safety fence far away from the sinful edge so that the danger of sin is remote.

THE ARGUMENT FOR THE WISE

If going to a party in Corinth and eating the food offered to idols were not sins, what was the problem? Paul gave three analogies to convince Christians in Corinth of a key wisdom principle. The principle arises from Paul's use of the word *participation* (*sharing in* as in the NASB) in 1 Corinthians 10:16–20. The word *koinonia* evokes the idea of Christian fellowship in the minds of many Bible students. The word may be translated "fellowship," but in this context the word draws on a deeper nuance of meaning. The word suggests an inward, spiritual communion between two entities that identifies each one as belonging to the other, a *sharing in* one another. We can derive a principle to guide our decisions from this term: *to participate is to have fellowship, and to have fellowship is to be identified with the other entity.*

Wise Christians realize the danger of participating in a certain action or activity. For example, some of the activities associated with the observance of Halloween in American culture have direct associations with the satanic and the demonic. Perhaps our participation in Halloween activities has some parallel to the issue in the church at Corinth. Paul's argument addressed the danger of associating with the demonic, even though the meat offered to idols and the idols themselves had no innate moral qualities. Paul illustrated three ways to substantiate the principle of participation and to encourage wise application to the situation in Corinth.

The first analogy involved Christians' participation in the Lord's

Supper, sometimes referred to as Communion. Paul said, "Is not the cup of thanksgiving for which we give thanks a participation in the blood of Christ? And is not the bread that we break a participation in the body of Christ?" (1 Cor. 10:16). To participate in the Lord's Supper is to have fellowship with the Lord and to be identified with him. The same principle holds true for our relationship with other members of the body of Christ as we take part in Communion (1 Cor. 10:17).

The second involved Israel's participation in sacrifices (1 Cor. 10:18). A sacrificial offering was usually divided three ways. The first part was offered to God, the second part was for the priest, and the third part was for the offerer to eat. By eating what was sacrificed, the participant identified with God. Was Paul saying that the meat offered to the idols in Corinth had the same significance as Old Testament sacrifices? Paul anticipated this question and then answered it: "Do I mean then that a sacrifice offered to an idol is anything, or that an idol is anything? No, but the sacrifices of pagans are offered to demons, not to God, and I do not want you to be participants with demons" (1 Cor. 10:19–20).

The third analogy involved the temple feasts in Corinth. Paul did not want Christians to be in *koinonia* with demons. By participating in the temple parties and enjoying a leg of lamb, Christians put themselves into the dangerous position of identifying themselves as belonging to demons rather than belonging to Christ and to God.

The core of Paul's argument is danger by association. The danger for Christians who participate in any given activity does not arise from their association with sinners, but from their identification with sinful actions. Paul's appeal was to flee from idolatry not from idol worshippers.

The wise person stops to consider this key principle when debating an issue like participating in Halloween. *To participate is to have fellowship, and to have fellowship is to be identified with the other entity.* Some of the harvest themes associated with Halloween seem harmless, but other aspects have a more direct association with the demonic. Where do we place the safety fence regarding Halloween? Christians' decision may differ as they apply wisdom. Let us give one another room to disagree, but the wise Christian will be sensitive to the wrong associations that Halloween may provoke.

THE ALTERNATIVES FOR THE WISE

Paul gave two basic alternatives to the Corinthians for the application of wisdom. Either do not participate in activities that identify with the demonic or end up provoking the Lord to jealousy. In 1 Corinthians 10:21 Paul said, "You cannot drink the cup of the Lord and the cup of demons too; you cannot have a part in both the Lord's table and the table of demons." Christians have to realize the implications of their choices. We should not observe the Lord's Supper on a Sunday, expressing identification with the Lord, and then on Tuesday participate in some activity associated with the demonic. Otherwise, we provoke the Lord to jealousy (1 Cor. 10:22a), and he has the right to be jealous because he is the only one who deserves complete allegiance and devotion. When a believer takes part in activities identified with the demonic, he or she provokes God to jealousy because he or she does not give the Lord the whole-hearted allegiance that he deserves.

Did not the Lord Jesus eat with sinners? Yes. Jesus Christ was strong enough to be able to handle any of these difficult situations without sin. Paul questions the wisdom of our assuming that we have the same strength. "We are not stronger than He, are we?" (1 Cor. 10:22b NASB). The expected answer is "No, we aren't." Christians who think they are strong enough to walk close to the edge of danger may not be wise.

Each neutral issue calls for a Christian to apply wisdom in decision making. Churches that are full of members who understand that where to put the safety fence may vary from person to person will be churches free to disagree agreeably and to allow different applications of wisdom. They will love and accept those in the congregations who may lack wisdom. Let us love one another enough to not lure the weak too close to the immoral edge. Let us avoid being foolish cliff walkers.

For Lively Discussion

1. What if an unsaved co-worker invites you to have a drink after work? What if a neighbor invites you to a heavy metal rock concert? Should you go?
2. How would you counsel the fellow Christian who has a history of gambling addiction in relation to his planned business trip to Las Vegas?
3. What area in your life as become a "danger zone" for you? What practical ways show your "safety fence" to be a wise, sensible distance from your "danger zone"?
4. What would your counsel be to a fellow Christian who has no personal problem with your "danger zone"?
5. Where should the "safety fence" be placed in relation to Halloween?

1 Corinthians 10:23–30

"Everything is permissible"—but not everything is beneficial. "Everything is permissible"—but not everything is constructive. Nobody should seek his own good, but the good of others. Eat anything sold in the meat market without raising questions of conscience, for, "The earth is the Lord's, and everything in it." If some unbeliever invites you to a meal and you want to go, eat whatever is put before you without raising questions of conscience. But if anyone says to you, "This has been offered in sacrifice," then do not eat it, both for the sake of the man who told you and for conscience' sake—the other man's conscience, I mean, not yours. For why should my freedom be judged by another's conscience? If I take part in the meal with thankfulness, why am I denounced because of something I thank God for?

— *8* —

Dinner Parties with Unbelievers

When I was a pastor in the Dallas-Fort Worth area, I officiated at more weddings than I do now as a professor at Multnomah Biblical Seminary. I enjoyed the beauty, pageantry, and jubilant surroundings that energized me. I looked forward to guiding couples through crucial issues in premarital counseling sessions. I liked to listen to the couple's desire for a Christian wedding.

One couple, Daryl and Sue, satisfactorily completed the required number of premarital counseling sessions. I felt reassured by their Christian testimony and by our planning together. I knew that Daryl wanted to present a clear testimony to his unsaved family during the message portion of the wedding.

Weddings I like. Rehearsals I endure because they often present awkward moments. The challenge at the rehearsal is to introduce complete strangers to each other so that everything can be coordinated into a smooth, attractive wedding ceremony for the bride and groom. Daryl's and Sue's Friday night rehearsal went well. Afterward, we went to a restaurant for the rehearsal dinner.

My wife and I conversed with Daryl's and Sue's family and friends at the dinner, paid for by Daryl's folks. Several people began drinking before the salad was served. While the waitress made her way toward us with what I assumed to be a fine vintage of wine, my wife was immersed in conversation with the person next to her. Neither one of us had ever touched a drop of alcohol. Both of us were raised in Christian homes by parents who believed that drinking any alcoholic beverage would be wrong. My church youth group trained me long ago to be polite in my refusal and to ask for an alternative. When the waitress came to me and reached to fill my glass, I caught her eye. Quietly I said, "Could I have some iced tea instead, please?"

"Sure," she said as she moved around me to my wife.

"She will have some iced tea, too," I said. "Thank you." My wife glanced back briefly and nodded agreement, then continued her conversation.

I looked around to see who might be watching us. No one was. Then I watched as the waitress proceeded to fill the everyone else's wine glasses. I did not see anyone stop her. She probably poured the wine freely for everyone else present. Suddenly I felt out of place and fearful. Maybe the rehearsal dinner might develop into an out-of-control, embarrassing party. I mentioned my observations to my wife when I had the chance. I knew that she would have begun to feel some of the same discomfort.

Daryl and Sue introduced everyone, and we continued in pleasant conversation with those around us while we enjoyed the delicious meal. Further into the evening, several people proposed a toast to the bride and groom, and we lifted our iced tea to each salute. At the appropriate moment, we said our good nights and slipped out. No harm done.

No one asked any questions. The wine flowed, and most of the guests drank in moderation. If the waitress had poured the wine into our glasses while we were away from our tables, we might have sipped some accidentally as if it were apple juice. I am not sure anyone would have cared if the pastor had sampled wine on that occasion. It did not appear to be an issue for anyone.

Weddings are occasions for celebration. Jesus accepted an invitation to a wedding in Cana of Galilee. When the guests ran out of wine, the Lord turned the water in six stone water pots into the best wine that the headwaiter had tasted all evening (John 2:1–11). The Lord's miraculous sign displayed the glory of the Son of God, and the guests at the wedding celebration enjoyed the results.

Had we sampled the wine at Daryl's and Sue's rehearsal dinner and someone who thought Christians do not drink wine had been carefully watching us, we might have been questioned about it. Suppose someone had said, "I didn't think pastors drank wine." The freedom that Jesus enjoyed in a particular social situation in his culture may not be the same as the freedom that I have in American society.

The Bible provides wise counsel for an occasion when someone at a dinner party questions whether a Christian should partake. It helps answer questions like:

"What if an unbeliever invites me to a private dinner party?"

"How do I decide when to stop enjoying my freedoms?"

"What practical principles about neutral issues can I use in daily life, especially if non-Christians may be watching me?"

The advice comes to us from the apostle Paul in 1 Corinthians 10:23–30. The first recommendation balances freedom and wisdom principles. Paul said, "'Everything is permissible'—but not everything is beneficial. 'Everything is permissible'—but not everything is constructive." The words *everything is permissible* must be understood in the context of the apostle's discussion of neutral or disputable issues, particularly eating meat sacrificed to idols. All neutral issues permit the strong Christian to participate without sin, although some of these things are not beneficial or constructive.

The Bible's advice here suggests two good questions to ask. First, will my participation be beneficial to me as well as to the lost? Life presents every Christian with a myriad of opportunities to enjoy freedom in Jesus Christ—some more beneficial to healthy Christian living than others. What is beneficial to one believer might be detrimental to another. If a Christian with diabetes joins a group at the local ice-cream parlor and the group orders a huge, rich conglomeration of pistachio, chocolate, and vanilla ice cream with assorted sauces and toppings, then the diabetic's choice to exercise freedom to eat will not be wise and certainly will not be beneficial.

As Christians, we also need to think about the disputed activity's effect on our testimony to the lost. If a nonbeliever does not associate the activity with sin, the Christian can participate. But if the nonbeliever relates the issue to sin, Christians should abstain. In any case, whether or not an activity is beneficial will differ for each Christian in each situation, and some will be more beneficial than others. When a strong person decides to participate in some neutral matter, the action itself has no moral consequence. We must remember, however, that what is merely good can be the enemy of what is best.

The second question is, Will my decision be constructive and spiritually uplifting? How will this decision help me? Not every decision in life has a direct spiritual consequence, but all of life can be governed by consciousness of God's presence. Our active awareness of the presence of the Lord in our lives will flavor our choices. My concern, however, must extend beyond myself. I must also ask how my decision will impact the lives of the people around me. Will my choices hurt someone? More than that, will my decision help or uplift someone? Let us say that the debated point would not hurt anyone and might even be beneficial. Paul's next word of wisdom is that we may participate with enjoyment. The Corinthian Christians wondered if they should proceed to eat the meat served at a dinner party, even if there was a chance that the meat had been offered to idols in the pagan temple rituals. What does the Lord say through the apostle? "Eat anything sold in the meat market without raising questions of conscience, for, 'The earth is the Lord's, and everything in it'" (1 Cor. 10:25). The Bible thus counsels that we participate without asking questions. The Bible tells the strong Christian to enjoy the meal. If an unbeliever invites you and you want to do it, go for it! Assume the best. Why ruin a good meal? Why put a relationship in jeopardy? The food is clean, for "the earth is the Lord's" (1 Cor. 10:26).

Some Christians today insist that in order to enhance our fellowship with God, we should be vegetarians or to abstain from certain foods. According to 1 Timothy 4:1–5, this particular teaching reflects demonic, earthly wisdom because "everything God created is good, and nothing is to be rejected if it is received with thanksgiving" (1 Tim. 4:4). Some people are advised by doctors to adhere to a strict diet for physical reasons, but requiring a vegetarian diet for spiritual purposes promotes unhealthy doctrines. As a strong Christian, you may eat anything with anyone anywhere you want to go, especially if you accept the fact that you are a missionary and are to reach the lost around you.

What if someone at the table or at the dinner party says, "Christians don't eat that, do they?" Then the whole situation changes. The Lord's wise counsel tells us not to eat it. Notice Paul's words to the Corinthians. "If anyone says to you, 'This has been offered in sacrifice,' then do not eat it, both for the sake of the man who told you and for conscience' sake—the other man's conscience, I mean, not yours. For why should my freedom be judged by another's conscience?" (1 Cor. 10:28–29).

The strong Christian, then, can feel free to take part in the meal without violating his own conscience at all. If everyone around accepts the same freedom and no one questions it, then everyone may enjoy whatever food or drink is served. If someone in the group questions something, then the strong should not go ahead. Why? Because the one who asks the question might be an unbeliever who thinks that Christians do not participate. In this case, the Christian should abstain for the sake of the conscience of the one who raised the question. Otherwise the freedom of the strong Christian would be criticized and slandered. Why let something I enjoy and thank God for be condemned by someone else (see Rom. 14:16)?

Paul says, "If I take part in the meal with thankfulness, why am I denounced because of something I thank God for?" (1 Cor. 10:30). When some unbeliever questions my liberty or wonders aloud whether Christians "do things like that," God's Word counsels me not to do it. The context of Paul's instruction pertains to dinner parties with unbelievers. The principle of sensitivity to the conscience of the unbeliever keeps the strong Christian's freedom from unnecessary criticism and keeps the door open to an effective witness. Paul's example mentions the unbeliever who states "This is meat sacrificed to idols" as the food is being set in front of the believer. What happens if the strong believer begins to eat the meat and then the unbeliever says, "Oh, by the way, this is meat sacrificed to idols"? The same principle applies. The best choice might be to quit eating at that point and say something like, "I'm sorry. I didn't realize that."

The advice of God's Word in connection with unbelievers provides wisdom for our relationships in the body of Christ. Do we ask questions first to learn the personal convictions of fellow members of our local church? Or should we just proceed to enjoy our freedoms unless someone says something?

The answer depends on our level of familiarity. If someone whom we respect for maturity in the Lord has raised a question, we should be careful to study the issue to determine the wisdom of our decisions. If an unsaved person does not think the issue is sin but has heard Christians claim it is sin, we might want to explain the biblical reasons for our freedom in Christ. If an unbeliever is convinced that the issue is sin, a good Christian will abstain.

If we suspect that someone may question our freedom, why put our liberty in jeopardy? Why risk criticism or condemnation? More importantly, why risk their rejection of the gospel? If, however, I am afraid that I have not thought of every potentially damaging freedom, I could freeze up in borderline paranoia. This passage from 1 Corinthians 10 allows me to enjoy what I enjoy without worry. I need not worry about what other people may be thinking or feeling about an issue. However, when they say something, I must respond appropriately. In the area of neutral issues, I cannot be held accountable for what I do not know, but if I have reason to suspect a problem, wisdom suggests caution.

Most native Oregonians have become Portland Trailblazer basketball fans, and I am no exception. Fans without season tickets can see home games in either of two ways: They can sometimes get rare tickets to home games, but they have to sit in the "nosebleed" section of the basketball arena; or they can purchase "Blazer cable" and curl up in a chair with nachos to watch the game on TV. Since my family has better ways to spend money than either of those, I look for other ways to see important home games.

One way is to travel an hour and a half to visit my wife's folks. They have Blazer cable; thus they do not have to pay $15.95 per game, and my mother-in-law likes the Blazers. Besides, I need to visit them once in awhile.

I decided one Sunday-night game was worth watching. We called to make arrangements to go. My in-laws, however, impressed me with their support for their church. They wanted to attend the Sunday-evening service because their church was experiencing some trouble in the assembly. Because of this, we could not go, but I realized several factors were at work.

For over two years my wife and I had ministered in a church in Gresham, Oregon. This community church had asked me to preach on an interim basis and help out with the leadership. We enjoyed the people and the opportunities to minister. We also enjoyed our Sunday nights at home because the church had no Sunday-evening service. For us, attending Sunday-night church was not a mandate from God. It was after calling about the Blazer game that I realized that my wife's folks had been attending Sunday-night church services most of their lives. Whether they had the personal conviction that they should not ever forsake God's people or they did not want to miss the opportunity to support God's people through a very difficult time, they chose to sacrifice their enjoyment of a basketball game for the sake of others.

The disappointment that I felt in not being able to see the game was my problem. As a Christian who believed that I could be free to make the decision to watch the game, I should have realized that my in-laws might not have had the same freedom. I also realized that instead of becoming paranoid worrying about whether I should watch future Sunday-evening Blazer games, I can enjoy basketball games on Sunday evenings until they make known to me where they stand.

Whatever their reasons for refusing to allow us to watch the game that particular Sunday, my in-laws were gracious. They counterproposed a Friday-night game later on. Although we were not able to make it that Friday night, our relationship remained good. The Blazers played well that Sunday night without my watching!

For Lively Discussion

1. What principles guide our practical daily living in relation to neutral issues if non-Christians may be watching us?
2. In relation to our unsaved friends and work associates, if we are a strong Christian and we want to go to the company party, should we go?
3. What if we participate with unbelievers in a social situations and somebody says, "I didn't think Christians did that sort of thing." What should we do?
4. The advice of God's Word in connection with unbelievers could provide some wisdom for our relationships in the body of Christ. Should we ask questions first to learn the personal convictions of fellow members of our local church, or should we just go ahead and enjoy our freedoms unless someone says something?

Matthew 18:1–14

At that time the disciples came to Jesus and asked, "Who is the greatest in the kingdom of heaven?" He called a little child and had him stand among them. And he said: "I tell you the truth, unless you change and become like little children, you will never enter the kingdom of heaven. Therefore, whoever humbles himself like this child is the greatest in the kingdom of heaven. And whoever welcomes a little child like this in my name welcomes me. But if anyone causes one of these little ones who believe in me to sin, it would be better for him to have a large millstone hung around his neck and to be drowned in the depths of the sea. Woe to the world because of the things that cause people to sin! Such things must come, but woe to the man through whom they come! If your hand or your foot causes you to sin, cut it off and throw it away. It is better for you to enter life maimed or crippled than to have two hands or two feet and be thrown into eternal fire. And if your eye causes you to sin, gouge it out and throw it away. It is better for you to enter life with one eye than to have two eyes and be thrown into the fire of hell. See that you do not look down on one of these little ones. For I tell you that their angels in heaven always see the face of my Father in heaven. What do you think? If a man owns a hundred sheep, and one of them wanders away, will he not leave the ninety-nine on the hills and go to look for the one that wandered off? And if he finds it, I tell you the truth, he is happier about that one sheep than about the ninety-nine that did not wander off. In the same way your Father in heaven is not willing that any of these little ones should be lost."

— *9* —

Slow: Children at Play

A FOUR-YEAR-OLD girl decided to pack some of her things into a sack and leave home. She carried her stuff out the door and stopped at the curb. She set down her load and looked at the street. Then, she picked up everything, followed the sidewalk one block to the next intersection, turned to her right and kept going. She walked around the block several times until a friendly policeman stopped her. "What are you doing?" he asked.

"I'm running away from home," she said.

"Why are you going around the block?" he asked.

"Because Mommy and Daddy told me never to cross the street."

While we smile at that old joke, we also know the value of instilling into our young children certain standards, rules, and convictions. Little ones need the guidance and protection of caring adults. But when will it be appropriate for this little girl to learn that legally crossing the street is not wrong? In most homes, a child cannot cross the street alone until she has permission from her parents. If she were to cross the street without her parents' consent, she would sin because she would have disobeyed her parents.

An awkward moment may come, however, on the first day her parents encourage her to walk three blocks to her school. If this conscientious little girl is never given permission to cross the street, she might be confused at the first curb. If she were to go ahead and cross the street, she might feel some guilt or a rush of excitement because she did something that she had been told not to do, even though it was in order to do something else she was told to do—walk to school.

As a parent, I repeatedly told my daughters not to do many things for their safety when they were small children. "Don't touch that outlet!" "Don't go into the street." "Don't touch the stove." I am amazed that my daughters do not struggle more with electrical appliances, driving, and cooking!

Mom's and Dad's rules usually change as kids grow older. Parents sometimes try to explain the changes, but complexities mount when brothers and sisters at different age levels have different rules and standards. When the oldest child approaches preadolescence and adolescence, some parents start to add standards and rules that they feel will guard their teenager from various dangers. Common rules include a curfew time and a minimum age requirement before they may go out on a date. Christian parents sometimes project fear while they heap rules on the preadolescent. Meanwhile the "Why, Mommy?" question becomes much more sophisticated, and the "because Mommy says so" answer becomes less and less effective as teenagers want solid reasons and good thinking.

SOME DANGERS

One of the big dangers that parents face occurs when their teenager challenges the thinking behind parents' convictions and rules. Some parents slip into a legalistic mode and force their children not to ask questions or challenge their rationale. If Mom or Dad sternly insist on the rules in a legalistic manner, then the parents' pharisaical attitude may frustrate the teen so much that he or she inwardly rebels and moves further toward bad decision making. Thus, a stifling, overprotective, legalistic atmosphere in the home is one danger.

Another danger occurs when the dependent, trusting child is trying to grow into an independent, critically thinking adult. This characteristic, normally associated with preadolescence or adolescence, poses special challenges for parents. Most parents want their children to grow up and think for themselves, but not if it means questioning the personal convictions of Mom and Dad in areas of neutral issues. Most Christian parents feel that certain neutral issues are wrong for them and their children, and they probably feel certain that other issues are very unwise. Typically, Christians want standards of behavior to be black or white, right or wrong—simplified. The spiritual life, however, cannot be reduced to such simple categories when the Bible allows for complex differences.

Our children deserve Bible-believing parents whose mature

thinking enables them to move from concrete thinking to abstract thinking, from treating all decisions as either right or wrong to recognizing amoral choices that require wisdom in order to know the best alternatives. Decisions regarding neutral issues require wise parents to teach the young, budding adult to make wise decisions.

A third area of danger erupts when one family disagrees with another family on how to raise children. Church families have lively discussions about neutral issues. Should I send my kids to a Christian school or a public school? Should I home school my children? Mature thinking allows for disagreement. Wise, mature parents will make their decision based on what they feel is best for their own children and will allow others to do what is best for their families.

Some parents have strong feelings about the importance of providing children's church or children's worship. Others feel that their children should learn how to worship with adults and how to sit quietly and reverently in the worship service. Still others feel that children should have something tailored for their age level within the adult worship service because kids should not be expected to have a good attitude about sitting with their parents when they do not understand or enjoy adult worship.

What is wise for one family may not be wise for another family, and no parent sins when a decision is made about the children's participation. Those who promote or lead a children's-church ministry will not be discouraged by a lack of participation if they understand the different perspectives. Parents who want their children to worship with them in adult worship should feel the freedom to make the decision without denunciation from anyone. Neither should they denounce the children's-church ministry.

A fourth danger is the issue of disciplining children, which often divides Christians. The Bible says a little more about child discipline than it does about children's church, but the Bible also leaves vast areas for wise choices to be made by parents. What form of discipline will we use in our home? Will we spank? If we spank our children, when should we start? Will we use our hand? A switch? A wooden spoon? How will we discipline our teenager? On and on the debate goes. Raising kids requires common sense, discernment, and insight. Parents who disagree with other parents learn to cooperate by allowing differences rather than by denouncing one another.

Parents who want to do what is best for their children in the areas of neutral issues refuse to flaunt their freedoms at the expense of their children. They heed the caution sign for home living—"Slow: children at play."

A HINT OF INSIGHT

American social standards regarding two neutral matters reflect how dangerous some adult liberties are for our children. Children's attendance at certain movies is restricted by agreements set up by the industry. The nomenclature of the movie rating system itself hints at the importance of protecting young children. A PG-rated movie urges parental guidance about whether children should see the movie. A PG-13 rating discourages parents from allowing a child under age thirteen to see the movie. The rating NC-17 disallows any child under seventeen years of age.

Legislation also prohibits minors from buying alcohol. American society has recognized the dangers related to the consumption of alcohol and for the most part has placed this drug off limits for anyone under the age of twenty-one. If our secular society recognizes the danger, Christians should take the hint.

Christian families and churches can learn an important principle from these societal norms. Although God's Word may allow freedom, let us exercise caution in regard to neutral issues to protect our children from harm. Responsible adults skillfully instill Christian convictions in children. God's educational plan puts the responsibility on the parents, not the church (see Deut. 6:4–9). The parents' job is to live the reality of their relationship with God in the home. The model of a life in love with Jesus Christ leaves an unforgettable impression in the mind of a child.

When a parent's mind and heart overflows with scriptural truth the best teaching occurs. Timothy's mother, Eunice, did an excellent job of teaching him the Bible from infancy (2 Tim. 1:5; 3:15). Timothy not only learned biblical truth, but he was convinced of it (2 Tim. 3:14). God's educational curriculum makes the Bible the central factor in shaping a child's worldview. We started our girls at a very young age on Bible memory work using simple Bible phrases that began with each letter of the alphabet. Right after dinner, I announced, "family time," and our daughters hurried into the front room. First, I opened the song box, and each member of the family reached in to grab a slip of paper with a children's song title. After singing and a very short Bible story either with pictures, puppets, or a drama by Mom and Dad, the girls recited their Bible phrases and references from memory. Later, we expanded the phrases to verses. Eventually they memorized whole paragraphs or chapters.

Churches provide Bible memory verses with Christian-education curriculum, and these provide parents with an excellent resource for teaching kids to learn God's Word. Parents cannot start too early but they can demand too much. We geared everything to our daughters' age levels, and we kept prayer times short. We usually closed our family time with fun time geared for the kids. We played games, rode bikes, went to the park, or did whatever was fun for them.

Formal teaching times as a family are good, but the best teaching occurs when parents seize teachable moments and events. We tried to recognize times when our daughters were ready to hear how God related to a situation. If one of our little girls noticed a pretty flower, I might say something like, "Isn't that a pretty flower? God made it!" If one of them asked a question, and I could think of a way to relate it to spiritual things, I did. I also did not want to force spirituality into their lives, but I did want them to feel a natural link between life and the Lord.

Not only did we want to raise a consciousness of God in our daughters, but we also wanted to teach them the essentials of God's Word. Some of these essentials were: God is the one who made everything; God loves us very much; Jesus Christ is God's Son; Jesus died on the cross to take away our sin; and the Bible is God's Word speaking to us.

A Christian parent also teaches children wisely in the area of nonessentials or neutral issues. Parents must define their own personal convictions on disputable matters. When a husband and wife disagree on an issue, they must disagree agreeably in order to decide which position to teach their children. Normally, the strong spouse defers to the mate who has no freedom to believe the issue is not sin. Strong family members defer to the weak, and this principle applies especially to children. Younger children deserve protection in areas of Christian liberty. American society already protects children in the areas of movies and alcohol and concerned parents may wish to be careful in other areas as well.

When children approach adolescence, however, wise parents will revise their standards on neutral issues to encourage the teenager to think through the issues. Smart parents will work hard to communicate the reasons for revising standards. One reason for revising a childhood requirement centers on the difference between nonessentials and essentials in Christian living. Thinking teens raised on Scripture will begin to wonder anyway. Why not guide early adolescent thinking on these issues before losing credibility with the teen?

As the teen matures he or she is able to discern what is healthy from what is unhealthy. Wise parents have been developing a sense of responsibility in them so their teen will be able to make good decisions. A teenager whose mind is saturated with God's Word will be better equipped to make wise choices. I remember the day when my older daughter, Joy, asked me whether she could go to the prom in her public high school. All through their elementary education we taught our daughters not to dance. We even sent special requests to excuse them from dancing in physical education classes. We gave our girls the usual reasons for not dancing, so they could answer the inevitable questions from kids at school. Although we did not believe dancing was sin, we did think it was unwise.

When Joy asked me about the prom, I realized she wanted to go with her boyfriend, a fine Christian young man (whom she eventually married). I knew my own conviction would not allow me to dance, but I also knew my daughter needed to develop her own conviction. She explained that the prom as a special occasion to dress up and be together. She said most of the couples did not even dance—they just stand around and then go out to eat at a fancy restaurant (which sounded boring to me!). I listened, and then I explained my position. I clarified the difference between the weak and the strong on the issue, and I explained the Christlike attitude each side should have. Then I informed her that I would let her make the decision. I said, "If you decide to go, just don't tell me whether or not you danced" (I was hoping she might decide not to go). She went anyway.

I was delighted at the level of maturity she displayed, and the level of trust she had in me. She asked. She listened to me, and she trusted me to have a Christlike attitude toward her even if she did dance. She made her own decision. To this day I do not know whether she dances, but I do know that she felt released to make her own decision and to enjoy her freedom in Christ.

One of the marks of true greatness is to humbly help God's people avoid sin. The Lord Jesus used a little child to illustrate this truth when he cautioned his disciples against causing a child to stumble in sin (see Matt. 18:3–14). True greatness comes through childlike humility that realizes the importance of removing whatever might cause spiritual damage to someone else, especially children. Children need adult protection that is provided without communicating a sense of legalistic alarm.

I took my two preadolescent daughters to visit a particular church one Sunday. We enjoyed the worship and the exhortations from God's Word. Then the Communion elements were served.

Since the church practiced open Communion, I whispered encouragement to my girls to participate. When the tray arrived, each of us took the element and ate it. They did the same with the cup, and immediately returned the empty cup to the tray before passing the tray to the next person. I watched as my older daughter drank the cup, then my younger before I drank the cup. Much to my surprise, it burned all the way down. We were not used to having wine in the cup. I wondered what my two young daughters were thinking.

As we were driving home, I asked them what they had thought about the worship service. "It was fine," one said. A long pause followed. Then she added, "What was in the cup?" When I explained that it was wine, my daughters almost panicked. They thought they had sinned!

I sat thinking. *How should I respond? I cannot judge the church members to be sinners. I may disagree with their choice of communion elements, but I must watch out for my attitude! I must be careful of having a dogmatic attitude in areas where the Bible has no clear, direct command.*

So I said, "Some churches feel they should serve wine in the cup because they believe the Lord Jesus used wine when he first introduced the Lord's Table to his disciples."

I waited for their response, but they said nothing. Then I continued, "That was OK today because there is room for disagreement about whether it should be juice or wine." Still no response.

"And you didn't you anything wrong," I added. That is when they relaxed.

That occasion provided an early lesson about differences among churches and Bible-believing Christians. How we as parents respond to these differences will be remembered long after what we said we believe has been forgotten.

For Lively Discussion

1. As a parent (or adult around children), what freedom do you enjoy which might be harmful to the kids? What will you do to protect them?
2. As a parent, have you taught your own personal convictions regarding nonessentials to your children? If so, have you made a decision to teach your children how to make their own wise decisions in these areas?
3. As someone who grew up with certain standards, what nonessentials remain ingrained in your thinking?
4. If you are no longer living at home and have parents who

disagree with the personal convictions you have developed over the years, what should your attitude be toward them?

5. When a mother who home schools her children says that it is wrong for Christian parents to send their children to public schools, who may be sinning?

1 Corinthians 10:31–33

So whether you eat or drink or whatever you do, do it all for the glory of God. Do not cause anyone to stumble, whether Jews, Greeks or the church of God—even as I try to please everybody in every way. For I am not seeking my own good but the good of many, so that they may be saved.

— *10* —

What Good Will It Do?

JAMES REFUSED TO join the group to picket the abortion clinic. "I don't see what good it will do," he said. "The media will focus on some radical demonstrator who breaks the law, and those who demonstrate peacefully will get no coverage."

"But aren't you against abortion?" Tim asked.

"Of course," James explained. "I just think there must be a better way."

Tim doubted that there was a better way. "Like what?"

"I don't know. Maybe we should work more through the judicial system and put pressure on the Supreme Court," suggested James.

"Whatever," Tim said impatiently. "But meanwhile, we're going to do something about it right now." Tim left with some friends to picket an abortion clinic.

Who was right? Neither James nor Tim sinned because lawfully picketing an abortion clinic is morally neutral (even though both people believed that abortion is morally wrong). The question between these two people was not, "Who is right?" but "What is the best way to protest abortion?"

When a concern (or method, as in the scenario above) is morally neutral, people who do not make a good decision do not sin. If James refuses to picket an abortion clinic, he has not sinned. If Tim lawfully pickets the clinic, he has not sinned. One decision may be wise or advisable, but individual discretion is not equivalent to morality. So how does a Christian learn to make wise choices?

How does a strong believer who feels free to participate in a disputable matter make perceptive, healthy decisions?

When biblical principles saturate our minds, the Lord enables us to generate wise decisions in the neutral zone of the Christian life. Christians who have known the Lord for several years have certain questions or principles that influence their own thinking and guide their advice to others. Common sample questions are, "Does it glorify God?" "Does it give offense to someone?" and "What would Jesus do?"

DOES IT GLORIFY GOD?

Unfortunately, these typical questions become tangled in a web of clichés. For example, the Bible commands believers to "do . . . all for the glory of God" (1 Cor. 10:31b), but how can a common neutral action such as walking, driving a car, or word processing be done for the glory of God? The context of 1 Corinthians 10:31 places no limits on the kind or number of actions that can be done to glorify God, and bringing glory to God combines with thankfulness to God. Thus, driving a car or walking along are neutral actions that can bring glory to God if they are done with a thankful heart. Any common action can also be sinfully abused to bring dishonor to God. The danger of abuse frightens some believers away from any enjoyment of safe, neutral aspects of life.

DOES IT GIVE OFFENSE TO SOMEONE?

A second criterion often tangled in cliché involves offense. When someone is offended by anyone for any reason, the word *offended* implies that feelings have been hurt. When someone has been hurt by damaging words, careless actions, or some other lack of love, the offender should confess any sin and apologize to mend any broken relationships. However, some hypersensitive people, who have not been wronged, still claim to have been offended. A person who says, "Her attitude offends me," might really be revealing a critical spirit under the guise of being offended. I remember one man under church discipline for committing adultery who said to me as pastor, "Your whole approach offends me," as if the church leaders were the sinners. Yes, church leaders must follow God's Word with good attitudes when seeking to restore a fallen member. Yes, even flawless church discipline hurts. However, the hurt caused by biblical discipline is designed to heal and restore God's way (see 2 Cor. 7:9–10, 12).

Another difficulty with the does-it-offend criterion involves potential confusion whether an issue is essential or nonessential (doctrine or behavior). People who are offended or repulsed by the shed blood of Jesus Christ or by the narrowness of Christianity need to continue to feel offended. Jesus' listeners in his hometown were offended by him, and Jesus never apologized to anyone for teaching the truth (see Matt. 13:57; John 8:46). The Pharisees and religious leaders expressed feelings of frustration, hurt, and anger toward Jesus and his disciples when the traditions of the elders were violated (Mark 7:1–16). Jesus, though, ignored their charges of wrongdoing even though they felt offended by him. Thus, we learn from the Lord that some people who feel offended have not been wronged at all!

Even though the criterion of offending someone may not always apply, several Scripture references urge the strong to be careful not to offend others. "Give no offense either to Jews or to Greeks or to the church of God" (1 Cor. 10:32 NASB); "All things indeed are clean, but they are evil for the man who eats and gives offense" (Rom. 14:20b NASB). Most biblical commentators define *offend* as cause to stumble spiritually or cause to sin. "Be careful, however, that the exercise of your freedom does not become a stumbling block to the weak" (1 Cor. 8:9). Church people who love others will ask "Does it offend someone?" and wise church people discern the right use of this question.

WHAT WOULD JESUS DO?

A third common standard for decision making asks, "What would Jesus do?" This question works well for a person intimately familiar with the ways of the Lord Jesus. Christian parents, who want their children to think the way they think in any situation, will use this question. When parents think the way Jesus thinks, they are helping their children. However, when people apply their own faulty upbringing and personal prejudice to a situation, they could mislead. What we have decided that Jesus would do and what Jesus would actually do may not be the same thing.

Although these three common guidelines have often been misapplied, two other principles seem fundamental to decisions in the realm of neutral issues. One principle involves wisdom. What is the wise thing to do? This broad question assumes that the person has the ability to discern wisdom that comes from God. A better way to discern is to ask, "Would this be unwise or foolish?" If the neutral issue is obviously unwise or foolish, the matter is easier to decide. A second principle involves the importance of exercising caution. Romans 14:23 says in essence, "When in doubt, don't." Persons with suspicions about a neutral issue may have doubt about their own involvement. For example, few people wonder whether drinking juice is sin. If you have no question, enjoy it. Conversely, if you suspect that drinking wine is sin, your doubt advises you to abstain.

A word of caution may be in order. Not everyone who doubts, sins. Doubt sometimes results from healthy, critical thinking. Raising questions about a disputable matter will inevitably lead to a better decision. The principle of "when in doubt, don't" refers specifically to a person's lack of faith to believe that God permits some specific action.

There are numerous questions and principles from God's Word to guide our decisions in morally neutral matters. When Scripture has saturated and transformed our minds, our decisions will better reflect God's wisdom in the difficult neutral arena. For brevity and practical use, I have chosen several guidelines taken from the more direct contexts where Paul discusses behavior in morally neutral matters.

Every one of these guidelines require a subjective opinion. The wisdom leading to one person's viewpoint may not be the wisdom for another person's viewpoint. Your evaluation of any so-called neutral issue will be prejudiced by your personal conviction. If you are a weak Christian, you will perceive the disputable matters to be violating several of these principles. However, if you are strong on a matter, these guidelines are for you.

The guidelines function best when a Christian who is strong must make a wise decision. The strong person, not the weak, is the one who needs special wisdom in neutral matters. The weak person's decision has already been made. The weak person should not take part in a doubtful situation because participation by the weak would be sin.

Those who are strong enjoy freedom in Jesus Christ. We have seen how the strong usually make the best evangelists (see chapter 8), but they also face tremendous dangers and obligations. They carry the responsibility of wisely and sensitively deferring to others in love. In those areas where you are strong, you bear the burden for the spiritual impact of your liberty on yourself and the people around you.

For these criteria to be most helpful, be aware of your specific cultural context. A change in cultural setting will shift the answers to the relational guidelines. Christians in American culture could multiply the examples of disputable matters.

The first set of five pairs of questions may be used when making a personal decision that does not touch another person. The personal guidelines pertain primarily to matters of personal behavior, not to philosophical or methodological differences among Christians such as how to be most effective in protesting abortion, how to conduct the affairs of a local church, or questions of doctrinal nature.

Let's choose a commonly accepted issue in order to include as many readers as possible on the "strong" side of the neutral fence. For example, should you go snow skiing next Friday and Saturday?

Personal Guidelines

Negative Tests	Positive Tests
1. Will it tempt me to be led into sin? (1 Cor. 10:13–14; Rom.13:14)	1. Will it lead me away from the danger of sin?
2. Will it subject me to demonic attack? (1 Cor. 10:14–22)	2. Will it help me avoid demonic attack?
3. Will it prevent me from being able to thank God? (1 Cor. 10:30; 1 Thess. 5:18)	3. Will it enable me to give thanks to God?
4. Will it tempt me to become addicted? (1 Cor. 6:12)	4. Will it help me avoid addiction?
5. Will it harm my physical or emotional health? (1 Cor. 6:19–20)	5. Will it help my physical or emotional health?

You probably answered all categories "no," even on the positive side. If you did, you simply classified your snow skiing trip as neutral. You might have answered in the affirmative on positive test 3, "will it enable me to give thanks to God?" Snow skiing, after all, sometimes provides breathtaking views of God's creation that prompt praise to God.

You might have hesitated on negative test 5. Snow skiing, like many sports or activities, can be dangerous. Like many other activities (such as driving a car), reckless snow skiing becomes dangerous. However, abuse of something by someone else does not prevent your participation. Another possible complication might be your bad knee. After two major surgeries and warnings from different doctors, snow skiing may be permissible but very unwise for you. In this case, this one test determines wisdom for you!

Now let's shift our example to relational areas. Most decisions also affect others in some way. Your specific cultural context sets the boundaries of prudence for you, and your relational framework includes your family, friends, church, and community. Although some decisions are personal, other matters related to daily living directly involve others. For example, should you and your spouse sign up for a square-dancing class? This decision involves your spouse and others who attend the class. Test the decision with the following relational guidelines.

Relational Guidelines

Negative Tests	Positive Tests
1. Will it do spiritual damage to me or others? (1 Cor. 8:9–13; 10:23–24, 32–33)	1. Will it spiritually build up me or others? (Rom. 14:19)
2. Will it be discovered and condemned by another person's conscience? (1 Cor. 10:27–29; Rom. 14:16)	2. Will it be encouraged by others?
3. Will it bring dishonor to God? (1 Cor. 10:31; Col. 3:17)	3. Will it bring honor and glory to God?
4. Will it violate the pattern of a Christlike role model? (1 Cor. 11:1; Eph. 5:1–2; Heb. 13:7)	4. Will it provide a Christlike role model?
5. Will it bring dissension or disunity to the body of Christ? (Rom. 14:19–20; 15:2, 5–6)	5. Will it bring peace and unity to the body of Christ?

Having looked over the five pairs of relational questions, you might decide to take a square-dancing class, especially if the class is taught by the pastor's wife in your church's basement. If, however, you had some uncertainty with one or more questions, wisdom might advise you to abstain. For example, if you suspect the possibility of someone in your family discovering and criticizing your square dancing, you are cautioned not to take the class.

Let us choose another recent American phenomenon. Should you enter one of the national sweepstakes to win millions of dollars? Should you fill out the forms, buy several stamps, and mail in your entry? Most of us would consider this to be an obviously neutral issue, but how does buying stamps to enter a national sweepstakes differ from the more controversial purchase of one state lottery ticket? Traditionally, many American churches have viewed gambling as sin, and lottery tickets have been classified by most Christians as a form of gambling. If you have a history of gambling addiction, tests 1 and 4 warn you to avoid buying lottery tickets. On the other hand, if you have no gambling problem, you might decide to buy the lottery ticket after reviewing the guidelines. Even though no one else saw you buy the ticket, if you won a multimillion dollar jackpot, you would find it very difficult to keep your win a secret and avoid influencing others. The relational guidelines apply.

Because of the controversy over gambling and lottery tickets among Christians in America, the second relational guideline questions the wisdom of your buying a lottery ticket. If someone with a background of gambling addiction hears that you bought tickets or that you won millions of dollars, the former addict, being weak, may be tempted to follow your lead.

Let's apply these principles to nonpersonal concerns, such as philosophy or methods of church ministry, and consider a debate about adding a drummer to the Sunday morning worship service. Assume that you enjoy worship with a tasteful use of drums and you serve on a church music committee assigned to make a decision. Imagine one person on the committee who has serious apprehension about the wisdom of drums in morning worship. In this situation, the person on the committee who is against drums being added to corporate worship has no personal weakness in this area. In other words, the one who counsels against playing drums in morning worship is actually a strong Christian who has concern for any other church member who believes drums are wrong.

Since the concerned committee member had no specific names in mind, the music committee chose to canvass the congregation for personal opinions on adding a drummer to corporate worship. If a church has a plurality of leaders who know everyone in the church, the leaders may be in the best position to make a healthy decision. Even so, the leaders and the music committee may choose to communicate their plan to the whole congregation and invite a response. If no one raises a serious objection, the drummer could probably be included without objections.

However, if some people in the congregation express a personal conviction against playing drums in corporate worship, church decision-makers should at least delay the decision out of deference to the weak and for the sake of unity. Otherwise, nearly all of the relational guidelines could be violated.

For Lively Discussion

1. When someone says he or she has been deeply offended, what else do we need to know to respond wisely?
2. What is the potential danger of asking "What would Jesus do?" in order to decide whether to participate in something?
3. Choose a currently debated issue among the members of your church and discuss how the personal or relational guidelines may apply.
4. Which of the following questions involve guarding against violation of a biblical command and which do not?
   Would it be more wise not to participate?
   Will this be making provision for the flesh?
   Do I risk becoming addicted to this?
   Will my decision be discovered and condemned by another person's conscience?

2 Corinthians 12:20

For I am afraid that when I come I may not find you as I want you to be, and you may not find me as you want me to be. I fear that there may be quarreling, jealousy, outbursts of anger, factions, slander, gossip, arrogance and disorder.

— *11* —

Deadly Sins in Disagreement

WHICH ONE OF the following persons sins? Someone who

- fails to communicate with another person in a timely manner?
- lacks understanding about what to expect in a relationship?
- grumbles about another person?
- betrays a confidence carelessly in conversation?
- fears that others are talking behind her back?
- talks about others in a negative way behind their backs?
- is nicer to some people than others?
- preaches boring sermons?
- buys a state lottery ticket?
- changes church traditions?
- says something unkind?
- mishandles someone's need?
- claims another person causes relational problems?
- fails to do a good job in ministry?

Christians often complain about the deterioration of the American judicial system because most judges and juries seem to operate from a worldview that appears to have no objective standards of right and wrong. Ironically, Christians often approach neutral issues in much the same way, condemning what the Bible permits and ignoring what the Bible condemns. For example, one church staff member criticized a teenager for wearing a baseball cap into the church building while no one wanted to discuss what to do with other teenagers who engaged in premarital sex. In another church, the Christian education board argued policy over the use of VCR units while ignoring a Sunday school teacher who was living in adultery.

Christians may be more upset over dancing, movies, constitutions, music, philosophy of ministry, or other matters in the morally neutral realm than they are over the sins of quarreling, slander, gossip, or arrogance (2 Cor. 12:20). Meanwhile, the deadliest sins creep into churches unnoticed. The Bible, not church members or church policy, identifies that which is sinful. A church that splits over a nonessential has completely missed the real sin taking place in their midst.

First Church members gathered at a congregational meeting to discuss whether tickets to the sweetheart banquet should be sold in the church building.

"No selling should be done in the church," said Tom in a settled tone of voice.

"I think it will be very hard to get people to come to the banquet unless we give them the opportunity to buy their tickets right after church," countered Ellen.

"When we allow money to change hands in our church, we make God's house a house of merchandise," Tom responded. "Jesus threw out the moneychangers to cleanse his Father's house. If we sell these tickets in the narthex, we are no better than those moneychangers in the temple," Tom continued, his voice becoming more forceful.

A third person tried to conciliate. "The problem was not the money that changed hands, but the transformation of the temple from a house of prayer to a place of financial corruption and greed by charging excessive fees for the exchange of foreign currency. Simply selling tickets for a banquet to promote loving marriages hardly seems corrupt."

"It's still buying and selling in God's house," insisted Tom. "I think you're confusing the temple with our church building."

Another church member had already discussed his point with several others before the meeting. "God doesn't dwell in a church building. He dwells in us."

"I'm on Tom's side," said Joe. "You people really disappoint me. Several of us have talked about this, and we all agree—the selling has to stop."

Jackie was upset. She jumped to her feet and pointed angrily at Joe. "I knew you were the problem. You have opposed our committee ever since you wanted to be on the committee and were voted down."

Joe shouted back. "I'm not the problem. Your insistence on committing sin is the problem."

"Are you calling us all sinners?" yelled Jackie.

Finally the moderator regained order and brought the heated discussion to an abrupt halt. "We need to have a motion before we have any further discussion," he said.

Attitudes continued to boil, hurtful words damaged relationships, the vote was taken, and most of the families of the defeated group left what they believed was a sinning church. The remnant of both groups at First Church continued to cause trouble for one another in the church.

The angry, hurtful words and the eventual split of the congregation at First Church were the true sins because selling tickets in a church building is a disputable matter. The Bible permits both groups to have a personal conviction about what is right, but the Bible condemns the attitude reflected by the critical, angry, and hurtful words that were said.

We are free to disagree, give our side, or dissent, but we are not free to disagree in a manner that causes disruption, disunity, divisions, or dissensions in our local church. Even when heretical teaching threatens God's flock, the Lord's servant must not be quarrelsome but kind to all and patient when wronged (2 Tim. 2:24). Heresy in basic doctrine calls for church discipline that gently corrects and warns the heretic (2 Tim. 2:25; Titus 3:10–11). If a disciplined heretic has loyal followers, the church may lose members in a split. Division always hurt a church, but when members argue over essential teachings, any resultant separation may protect sound doctrine.

However, many churches divide over peripheral doctrines. In the realm of disputable doctrines, any person's belief or conviction becomes secondary to maintaining unity in the bond of peace. Christians argue many different opinions about divorce and remarriage, spiritual gifts, the ordinances, the type of church government, elements for the Lord's Supper, or the kind of music in corporate worship. Churches seem to find no end to the topics about which to argue. Disagreements can be like the sun. The proper amount of light can make for healthy growth. Too much can devastate everyone like a burning desert. Sometimes healthy discussion and disagreement eventually becomes so hot it wilts relationships. In neutral domains, the preservation of healthy affiliation with others must outweigh personal conviction.

For example, if I disagree with you about some nonessential, nonmoral matter, my attitude toward you is more important than my opinion. The key to unity between us is humility. Humility regards the other person as more important than oneself, and humility looks out for the interest and perspective of the other person (Phil. 2:3–4). If I insist on my view without regard for your feelings, I may hurt you and ruin our friendship.

Healthy churches come to conclusions that originate in the adequate discussion of opposing viewpoints. Churches have a model of dispute resolution in Acts 15, when Paul and Barnabas had "sharp dispute and debate" with some believers from the party of the Pharisees. The church leaders gathered and debated the question of requiring circumcision for salvation, and they concluded that circumcision was not necessary. Their conclusion brought help and healing to the churches.

Beneficial conflict, however, turns sour when someone sins. Bitterness, anger, slander, and other injurious words damage relationships. Although any sin harms members of the body of Christ, there are several deadly sins that are usually ignored when controversy heats up regarding disputable matters.

Paul lists some of these sins in 2 Corinthians 12:20: "For I am afraid that when I come I may not find you as I want you to be, and you may not find me as you want me to be. I fear that there may be quarreling, jealousy, outbursts of anger, factions, slander, gossip, arrogance and disorder."

The sins that I have selected for this discussion are grouped under the categories of hurtful words, sinful attitudes, and divisive actions.

HURTFUL WORDS

Angry words directed at someone in a church business meeting injure both the person at whom they are directed and relationships. Most Christians recognize the sin in angry outbursts. Much more subtle is the deadly damage is done by the hurtful words that are said behind someone's back through the gossip and slander that flow freely among church members. Few people try to stop gossip, and fewer still handle gossip as sin.

"Malicious gossip" or "slander" is what the Greek word *diabolos* means. Gossip is one of the "diabolical" schemes that enables the enemy of our souls to ruin churches. Gossip slips into the informal agendas of parking lot meetings and telephone conversations. The sin of gossip occurs when a person gives an unauthorized, distorted, or false report that influences another person to form a bad opinion about the person being talked about. The Bible labels gossip and slander (or "reviling") as a sin that characterizes the life of the unbeliever (2 Tim. 3:2–4; Rom. 1:29–30; 1 Cor. 6:10) and as a sin for which a Christian should be disciplined (1 Cor. 5:11).

The *diabolos* way is sowing disagreement by spreading unauthorized, unsubstantiated information. Saying things that make another church member sound like a sinner, or even look bad, only proves that the person who says these things is the sinner. God's way to deal with sin in the congregation involves careful steps of church discipline outlined in Matthew 18:15–18 (see also 1 Tim. 5:19–21; Titus 3:10–11; Gal. 6:1). Church leaders and teachers fortify the congregation when members learn to deal with sin and disagreement in God's way instead of the *diabolos* way.

A word of explanation is in order though: Sometimes the apostle Paul gave ugly descriptions of people he called "false teachers," but what Paul was doing was not sin. Merely casting a person in a bad light is not necessarily wrong because an authorized warning may be accurate and very much needed for the protection of fellow members of the church.

Problems arise in the area of hurtful words when we fail to make sure that (1) the facts are right; (2) scriptural steps are taken toward those involved, (3) this is the authorized person to give the report, (4) the information is given to the appropriate persons, and (5) the information is given for the right reasons.

We have to be very careful if we think that we are hearing gossip from a spiritual leader whom God has placed over us. If the facts are right, this leader is the person who should be telling us, and he or she is telling us for the right reasons, then no sin is committed. That which makes gossip a deadly sin is the fact that it creeps into innocent conversation before anyone realizes it. I suggest that the following questions be asked to detect gossip or slander:

- Why are you telling me this?
- Where did you get this information?
- Have you gone to the people named?
- Have you personally checked out all the facts?
- Can I quote you if I check this out?

When someone refuses to answer one of these questions or the answer suggests that the person has something to hide, the listener has reason to suspect gossip. Perhaps each church member should write these questions out on a card and post it next to the telephone. The reminder just might be the dam that holds back the rampaging river of gossip.

SINFUL ATTITUDES

A second category of deadly sins includes a condemning spirit, selfish ambition, and envy, all of which are sinful attitudes. What makes these sins deadly is the difficulty that we have in being able to accurately recognize them. It's difficult to honestly discern our own attitudes, much less those of others. How do attitudes shift from virtuous to sinful?

Attitudes shift to sin when a person inwardly wishes either to harm or degrade another or to promote self. Christians who want others to admire them slip easily into selfish ambition at the expense of others. The desire to be respected pushes some people into defensiveness in discussion and debate. Any unloving attitude becomes obvious when someone carelessly abuses or wounds another person.

The first of these sinful attitudes is a critical, condemning spirit. When Christians, who have a dispute, begin to judge and condemn each other, they sin. The apostle Paul urged the strong and the weak in the church in Rome not to judge each other when they opposed one another in the exchange of personal opinion about nonmoral concerns (Rom. 14:3, 13; cf. Matt. 7:1–2).

Not all judging is wrong, however. The word *judge* refers to the importance of being able to discern—to judge at some competition, like Olympic springboard diving, gymnastics, or even at the county fair. Another place for positive judgment is in a courtroom. Even the apostle Paul is amazed that the church in Corinth had no one in the church qualified to judge between believers so that Christians had to take their cases to secular courtrooms (see 1 Cor. 6). However, when a person's intent is to degrade, disgrace, or shame someone else, then judging becomes a sinful attitude. This is what Jesus meant when he said, "Do not judge" (Matt. 7:1).

Frequently, churches suffer under strained, agitated relationships among the congregation and its leaders. One of the toughest times to trust God and love one another is when problems exist between elected church officers and church members. When God's people undermine selected officers and ministry staff personnel, the work of the Lord suffers. God wants peace within any congregation, especially between the congregation and its leaders (see 1 Thess. 5:12–14).

The Scriptures present several responsibilities that church members have toward church leaders. First, we are to observe them enough to appreciate their work (1 Thess. 5:12; 1 Tim. 5:17). Second, we must hold them in high regard in love (1 Thess. 5:13). Third, we are to submit to them (1 Cor. 16:15–16; Heb. 13:17). Fourth, we are not to listen to people's accusations of them (1 Tim. 5:19) unless it is an accusation of clear sin and others can verify the sin. Fifth, we are to call on other church officials to wisely deal with any of God's leaders who have clearly sinned (1 Tim. 5:19–21). Congregations who are disturbed by a leader's abrasive or unwise actions must first ask whether someone has sinned. If no one has sinned, the debate falls into the realm of legitimate disagreement. A church member's attitude is more important than any person's perspective in such a dispute.

Thus, when congregations become upset because of poor judgment by those in positions of authority in the church, several factors will keep them from sin. First, regardless of how your church leaders are selected, they are God's appointed authorities for your congregation. Personal attacks, slander, and verbal abuse are not morally permissible. Second, God's appointed leaders sometimes do a poor job of leading. Submission to God-ordained authority does not depend on the quality of the official. Third, when a person feels that there is a problem with the preaching or teaching of a church leader, a personal word with that person, given with a loving, concerned attitude, is biblical (see Priscilla's and Aquila's interaction with Apollos in Acts 18:24–27).

The reverse side of putting others down is pumping up one's own self in the estimation of others. This second sinful attitude, selfish ambition, involves the desire to put one's self forward as better than someone else in a partisan or factious way. A politician wants to be projected as better than someone else in a partisan way, but Christians who use this tactic damage their local church.

Listed as one of the deeds of the flesh in Galatians 5:20, selfish ambition rears its ugly head in Christian ministries. The apostle Paul tells the Philippian church, "Do nothing out of *selfish ambition* or vain conceit, but in humility consider others better than yourselves" (Phil. 2:3, emphasis mine). He observes how some preachers "preach Christ out of *selfish ambition,* not sincerely, supposing that they can stir up trouble for me while I am in chains" (Phil. 1:17, emphasis mine).

The danger of selfish ambition intensifies in congregational meetings or in leaders' meetings when members elect officers or vote on controversial issues. The democratic format invites members to lobby for the promotion of their particular idea. While good resolutions depend on a thorough communication of reasons and alternatives, helpful discussion and debate can become dangerous when people are so personally attached to their opinion that any reasonable objection is perceived by them to be a personal attack. Lobbying for a proposal degenerates into lobbying for the promotion of the person. People can become defensive, pumping themselves up and putting others down. Their attitudes have shifted from cooperation to selfish ambition.

Attitudes intended to condemn others and promote self might be fueled by envy, the third sinful attitude. Envy resents someone else's advantage and secretly rejoices when another person loses benefits or prominence. Envy becomes more obvious when a person does or says things to degrade, demean, or destroy someone. The Bible says: "For where you have envy and selfish ambition, there you find disorder and every evil practice" (James 3:16). Envy caused the rebellion against Moses, caused Joseph to be sold into slavery, made Saul pursue David, and crucified Christ (see Matt. 27:18; Mark 15:10).

When people in leadership are elected for limited terms and rotated, those who rotate out face the frustration of losing the power and respect associated with a position of authority. Some handle it well. Others fight to regain influence through whatever means possible. Former elected officers in local churches often struggle with these sinful attitudes. Sometimes previous leaders try to influence the outcome of decisions that are made by their successors. Because they believe that their opinion helps the church or because they want more control, they will complain of inadequate communication and poor judgment by the leadership. Out of envy, they will undermine church officials by openly condemning them while seeking to promote their own opinion. Nothing justifies selfish ambition or the denunciation of the current leadership.

A critical spirit, selfish ambition, and envy provide a small sample of the dangerous attitudes that are possible when Christians differ. The sin is not the conflict or quarrel itself, but the argumentative attitudes that the Bible identifies as sin.

DIVISIVE ACTIONS

Beyond hurtful words and sinful attitudes, deadly sins in disagreement include dissensions, factions, and divisions (Gal. 5:20;

2 Cor. 12:20). Division involves the breakdown of the relationship between two or more people as a result of individual sin or unresolved disputes.

When conflict among church members ends in attitudinal or physical division, sin has ruined the local church. Does conflict have to end this way? Can we agree to disagree? As we have seen, opposing viewpoints are permitted by God if our demeanor toward one another preserves a harmonious relationship. Unity is primarily an attitude, a way of thinking and feeling toward one another. If we disagree, we must be kind. The Lord Jesus prayed for unity (John 17:11, 20–23). So did the apostle Paul, who both prayed for and urged unity (Rom. 15:5–6; 1 Cor. 1:10; Eph. 4:3). Unity comes before any personal opinion. Unity supersedes any agenda or proposal. The number one priority of church members is to maintain unity during controversial debates and potentially divisive decisions. Splitting the church is a deadly sin that denies the Bible's call to unity in the body.

Two divisive actions listed as "deeds of the flesh" in Galatians 5:20 include dissensions and factions. The NIV translates the word for *dissensions* as "divisions" in the only other use of the word in Romans 16:17: "I urge you, brothers, to watch out for those who cause divisions and put obstacles in your way that are contrary to the teaching you have learned. Keep away from them." When a person causes divisions in the church, that person has sinned.

Sometimes well-intentioned church officials fear division so much that they stifle any objections or opposing points of view. Leaders sometimes mistakenly suppose that any genuine difference of opinion will be divisive or cause dissension. Divisions result from defiant, condemning messages, both verbal and nonverbal that spring from a polluted well of bad attitudes. Wise church leaders allow for and encourage different perspectives and ideas, but when the rhetoric changes and becomes malicious, prudent leaders stay alert in order to alleviate tensions.

The second divisive result mentioned in Galatians 5:20 is factions. Six of the nine uses of the word occur in Acts, usually in reference to a "sect" or a "party." Paul uses the word one other time to describe the "differences" among the groups in the divided Corinthian church (1 Cor. 11:19). Teaching that results in a group separating from other members of the body of Christ is false teaching, not because it is untrue or undesirable but because it is divisive. The Bible urges that we measure sound, healthy teaching by the results it produces (see 1 Tim. 1:10; 6:3; 2 Tim. 2:16–18).

We have yet another factor to suggest the validity of applying principles of disputable matters to areas of doctrine. When respected, Bible-believing members of the body of Christ disagree, it signals the probability of a disputable, unimportant doctrine. In such cases, Christians of mature character eagerly study the Bible to form their opinions (see Acts 17:11). Even so, personal convictions should be secondary to unity because dogmatic insistence on a specific position or opinion shuts out Christians who disagree.

So, helpful doctrinal statements allow for greater agreement among members throughout the universal body of Christ. Trouble arises when local churches confuse peripheral doctrines with essential doctrines. Five questions for determining what is essential or nonessential have been mentioned in chapter 1. The fifth one is particularly appropriate for differences of opinion that might lead to division in the church: Would I die rather than renounce them as untrue or unnecessary for every believer? Thus, the author's required doctrinal statement is much shorter than those found in many churches.

Many of the differences separating American denominations involve peripheral tenets. Some local churches justify their separate existence by trumpeting minor differences in disputable matters. In a refreshing movement of the Spirit of God here in the Northwest, pastors of local churches join together for prayer and worship celebration in meetings called "pastors' prayer summits." Pastors from widely varying denominational groups major on the essentials and leave the rest behind. The resultant unity among these pastors is what the Lord wants for all the members of the body.

Blessed be the local churches that comprehend the distinction between disputable matters and deadly sin.

Deadly Sins in Disagreement

2 Cor. 12:20	Greek Word	Gal. 5:20
quarreling	ερις	discord
jealousy	ζηλος	jealousy
outbursts of anger	θυμοι	fits of rage
factions	εριθεια	selfish ambition
slander	καταλαλιαι	
gossip	ψιθυρισμοι	
arrogance	φυσιωσεις	
disorder	ακαταστασιαι	
	εχθραι	hatred
	διχοστασιαι	dissensions
	αιρεσεις	factions

For Lively Discussion

1. How do we discern the difference between strong feelings regarding what is foolish and the strong feelings regarding what is wrong?
2. Which one of the following words describes sin?
   brutal
   rash
   deceit
   obscene
   strife
   discord
3. How would you explain the *diabolos* way as described in this chapter?
4. How is it possible to judge others without sin?
5. What is the potential problem with having a fairly detailed doctrinal statement?
6. If a church leader does a poor job of leading or preaching, how should the situation be handled?

1 Thessalonians 2:7–12

But we were gentle among you, like a mother caring for her little children. We loved you so much that we were delighted to share with you not only the gospel of God but our lives as well, because you had become so dear to us. Surely you remember, brothers, our toil and hardship; we worked night and day in order not to be a burden to anyone while we preached the gospel of God to you. You are witnesses, and so is God, of how holy, righteous and blameless we were among you who believed. For you know that we dealt with each of you as a father deals with his own children, encouraging, comforting and urging you to live lives worthy of God, who calls you into his kingdom and glory.

— *12* —

Institutionalizing Neutral Issues

BACK WHEN BELL-BOTTOM pants and sideburns made a fashion statement, a young seminarian walked into a hardware store for a job interview. He wanted the position because the business was owned by Christians who were not ashamed of their relationship with Christ. Toward the end of the interview, the manager said, "We would love to hire you right away. As you may know, we employ only Christians, and we want everyone who works here to have an excellent testimony by the way they appear. If you want this job, you will have to cut your sideburns and not wear colored shirts."

The young man politely acknowledged the criteria, smiled, and said. "I will have to give it some thought. I'll be praying about this in the next couple of days. I'll let you know what I decide." As he left, he felt insulted to think that his Christian testimony was judged only by his appearance. He decided not to take the job.

Why was the student offended? Was it because he did not like the thought of wearing a "uniform"? Any institution or place of employment may set its own dress code. Fast-food restaurants often require a certain uniform for all employees. Even corporate executives are often urged to conform to certain standards of dress such as the familiar blue suit and white shirt. Sometimes technical or professional schools have regulations for the appearance of their students. The simple requirement for standards of appearance wasn't the real issue.

The manager's tone made the job seeker feel as though respectable Christians did not wear sideburns or colored shirts. Perhaps the seminarian felt obligated to resist legalistic thinking. When churches or Christian organizations require certain dress codes, they risk misleading people into thinking that their standards of appearance are more acceptable to God than that of other groups. Students, faculties, or employees of Christian institutions might think that a required dress code reflects God's standards for holy living, especially when the dress code is mixed with a list of sins from the Bible.

THE INSTITUTIONALISM OF CHRISTIANITY

The history of Christianity is filled with locations where the church once flourished but where it eventually lost the vibrancy of a vital faith. In each location, the blessing of God appeared to move to another region. Christianity migrated from Jerusalem to Antioch, then to Asia Minor and Macedonia, from Rome, to Europe, then on to America, and more recently to Third World countries. Initially, most of these regions experienced a wave of spiritual fervor followed by a steady deterioration of the churches.

One possible explanation for this phenomenon is Christianity's alliance with the state. In some regions, Christianity's impact on society, government, and culture became strong enough to dictate cultural norms, values, and standards. Christianity became more identified with certain political issues than with the cross-cultural principles of the Lord Jesus. When the political climate changed, Christianity's distinctiveness faded. The Bible warns the church not to lose its effectiveness by conforming to the secular culture (Rom. 12:2). James 4:4 says, "You adulterous people, don't you know that friendship with the world is hatred toward God? Anyone who chooses to be a friend of the world becomes an enemy of God."

A second possible explanation for Christianity's pattern of deterioration is the connection of Christianity with a specific cultural lifestyle. Broadly speaking, the early converts' enthusiasm for Christ resulted in a radical disassociation with the worldly culture in that particular region. Christianity became definable more by how Christians differed from the prevalent culture than by a cross-cultural commitment to biblical principles and the person of Jesus Christ. The problem for Christians is that the standards which define the culture shift over time. Thus, the Amish emphasis upon close families and agrarian lifestyles, while commendable in itself, has no impact on a culture that has moved well beyond the era of Model T

Fords versus the horse and buggy. A Christianity defined more by its rejection of a particular culture than by Scripture is headed for its own demise.

American Christianity has struggled with similar patterns. A Christianity identified with a certain political viewpoint or cultural lifestyle eventually fades. Mainline denominational churches, mostly identified with social liberalism, dwindled under the weight of a huge hollow shell of institutionalism. According to the Barna Research Group, since 1970 the Episcopalians lost 1.2 million, the Presbyterian groups lost 1.2 million, and the Methodists lost 1.6 million members.[1]

Individual local churches show a similar cycle of decline. Most local assemblies begin with dynamic fervor, rise to a peak of strength and effectiveness, then weaken and deteriorate. The major reason for this cycle may well be that Christians fail to grasp the reality of a living, moving, and transforming relationship with Jesus Christ and hold on instead to certain external behaviors and norms to define their church and their Christianity.

The pattern of decline also holds true in Christian families. The Christianity of parents may be passed on to the children in the form of rules for outward behavior. Because we all tend to live by sight and not by faith, our kids may recognize Christianity only by its outward and superficial standards. Parents who fail to encourage their children to think for themselves and internalize their faith may have the outward conformity of their children, but this conformity eventually leads to hollowness. As evangelist Luis Palau has often stated, God has no grandchildren. Each generation must have a saving faith in the work of Jesus Christ. Cautious parents will not force their kids into assuming that holy living is merely the choice to follow the parents' cultural preferences and patterns.

When Christians identify true Christianity more by its opposition to specific social norms than by the cross-cultural and timeless truths of God's Word, they risk losing the vibrancy of their faith. Christians indirectly institutionalize Christianity when their concern for the way members dress, the political views they hold, or the kind of music they listen to or use in worship outweighs their concern for inner holiness. Fossilization has begun. Thus, discussions and disagreements over nonessential matters need to be resolved in a manner that refuses to describe authentic Christianity merely by cultural norms.

A wise and discerning believer recognizes the real need to impact culture with the reality of a transformed life as well as the need to adapt to the changing cultural standards in the neutral arena.

Churches, Christian businesses, Bible colleges, and seminaries that are unwilling to change with the times in regard to these negotiable areas exacerbate the problem. Colleges and seminaries train future leaders in our churches, and they too frequently model a rules-oriented, externally motivated Christianity. In some schools, godliness appears to be equal to certain cultural norms adopted by aging faculties who designate holy living as separation from social features that are no longer important.

For example, some Christian institutions still forbid hand holding, card playing, musical instruments, and television. Other Bible colleges and seminaries allow students to play pool and card games in the student lounge area. Is holy living for a male seminarian still defined by white shirts, ties, and clean-shaven faces? Just as some cities and towns have outdated laws on the books, some Christian organizations also refuse to flex nonbiblical campus rules to change with the times. Of all the groups that should be open to change, Christianity's educational institutions should be leading the way.

Education assumes change. Hopefully, knowledge and learning bring beneficial changes in the students who are seeking to be transformed into the image of Jesus Christ. Yet, the fears of compromising doctrine, of moving away from the faith, or of conforming to "worldliness" cause Bible colleges and seminaries to oppose any restyling in legitimate adaptation to cultural changes. As a result, we too easily tumble into strife over nonessentials. The main things are no longer the main things. We strain at a microbyte and swallow a jumbo jet. We discuss the finer points that count for little while members of the body of Christ flounder in horrendous sins.

Institutional lists and requirements make externals appear to be a measure of holiness. We have forgotten that the Lord Jesus transforms the inner person, and we call attention to outward elements such as clothing, hair, or other lifestyle items instead. We tend to evaluate holiness by the way a person dresses, so we gossip about offenders.

We are reluctant to change Christian cultural norms because of the difficulty of change itself. Change produces tensions in fundamental areas of identity and acceptance in the body of Christ. If someone introduces a new song and I do not know the melody, I might feel weak and perhaps embarrassed by my inability to join in singing. If I cannot grasp the tune and I appear different from most of the group, I may feel left out. I may feel like I am in a different country, or I may fear that the group will not accept me with my different tastes or upbringing, treating me instead with some contempt.

The old familiar ways are more comfortable, less demanding,

and less time consuming. Christians who are stuck in a culturally bound Christianity want to ask, "Why do it differently when the old way works?" or "Why put myself into a potentially awkward situation?" Because culture changes, every Christian faces the challenge of adapting to different styles. Top hats, bell-bottom pants, leisure suits, and sports jackets without lapels died out years ago. Christians do not have to go to the mission field to encounter the difficulty of social fluctuation. Change occurs in our own country over a period of years. We need a missionary mentality to adapt to change at home.

INSTITUTIONAL WISDOM

How does an institution communicate wisdom in doubtful areas without giving tacit approval to weak Christians or without obscuring biblical principles of freedom? How do the weak and the strong relate to one another in such an institution? What wisdom guides an institution with children and/or teenagers?

Again, the Bible encourages the strong to defer to the weak (Rom. 15:1–2), and this principle applies to the policies of any Christian institution. Wisdom guides Christian institutions to encourage abstinence from questionable activities for biblical reasons while taking care not to communicate censorship if believers have the freedom to exercise their liberties in a careful, loving way in these same areas. Even more importantly, the weak must not become "legalistic" in these matters or in the enforcement of any institutional, nonbiblical standards.

One problem with deferring to the weak occurs when the institution's list of forbidden activities becomes so long it is impractical. Even within an institution, my biblical neighbor is the person who is close by. For this reason alone, a far better approach is to handle each situation individually through wise counselors rather than through the enforcement of a printed list.

In any institution that is preparing Christian men and women for ministry, complete training equips future leaders with an inner core of convictions that supplies mature wisdom for life. Most Bible colleges, seminaries, and churches want their students or members to defer in questionable activities, not because "the institution says so" in a legalistic fashion but because of the wise application of biblical principles. A better approach for churches and some higher educational institutions would be to teach wisdom principles in relation to neutral issues.

Lists and rules come about for various reasons. Usually, troublesome members of an institution provoke institutional policies, rules, and other devices to protect responsible leaders and decision-makers. Individual discipleship and counseling consume inordinate amounts of time, and rules streamline the process, freeing up leaders to minister to the needs of the whole group. Also, troublemakers refuse to submit to authority and often challenge any policies that they think are arbitrary and meaningless.

Some professing Christians file lawsuits. The fear of litigation induces leaders to write an objective standard and to want the protection of both a policy and a group decision. Abuse, however, should not dictate decision-making. The first recourse should be to confront in gentleness, teach with loving patience, and disciple in faithfulness those who abuse their love relationship with Jesus Christ and God's people. People are more important than policy. The apostle Paul spent the necessary time to disciple God's people. The apostle gave the Thessalonians more than knowledge; he gave them his own life. He treated them like a caring mother and a concerned father (1 Thess. 2:7–12).

Policies and rules can actually end up preventing an institution from effectively nurturing a hurting life. Christianity becomes measured by written statements and committee decisions. Life fails to touch life. Potential mentors hold troublemakers at arm's length. Institutional relationships leave hollow shells. Written guidelines can help if they are coupled with leaders who are more concerned with helping the person than enforcing a policy. Words of comfort, encouragement, and admonition are needed to put vibrant life into any institutional norms that are written on a piece of paper.

Most Christian homes face a transition similar to educational institutions. As children mature into adulthood, they need moral discrimination and wisdom to make competent moral choices independently. In developing mature thinking, Christians need to be motivated from the inside rather than from the outside.

For Lively Discussion
1. What are some of the factors which have led to the decline in the effectiveness of Christianity in various locations throughout church history?
2. What is the danger of a culturally defined Christianity?
3. What are some of the neutral issues which have shifted during your lifetime?
4. Discuss whether listing neutral things together with moral

issues is appropriate for Christian institutions such as Christian schools, churches, or parachurches.

CHAPTER NOTES

1. These data were taken from *The Church Today: Insightful Statistics and Commentary* (Glendale, CA: The Barna Research Group, 1990), 24, which also says, "Despite the consistent increase in the nation's population, church membership has declined among most Protestant denominations during the past decade."

Conclusion

A FORMER STUDENT of mine at Multnomah Biblical Seminary told a story which summarizes the way a neutral issue can become a problem among church members. I've changed the details, but the following story is based on an actual situation.

Almost every Thursday night a group of enthusiastic young adults went door-to-door to share the gospel. Several people were won to the Lord, and these new Christians were growing in the Lord through small home Bible studies. Eventually, some of these new believers decided that they wanted to be baptized. When the time came, the evangelistic team could hardly contain the joy they felt as they watched these young believers be baptized. After each person was baptized, the congregation would applaud the public stand they were taking for Christ.

After the first baptismal service, other new believers expressed interest in being baptized, so a second, and then a third baptismal service were scheduled. The group continued to clap after each person was baptized. When the last person in the third service had been baptized, the music leader got up to lead a song. A little offended by the spontaneous clapping, he motioned to the congregation to stop, and said, "Let this song be your response to the baptismal service."

The evangelistic team was shocked and greatly offended. How could he do that? Several team members became very upset and openly criticized the music leader immediately after the service. At a later meeting, the evangelistic team was told that the leaders of the church had discussed the issue. They had decided to appoint the music leader to take this action. This resulted in the team members directing their anger at the rest of the church leadership as well. Although the meeting ended with an agreement not to clap at baptismal services anymore, the anger in some team members took a long time to subside.

Some Christians in this particular church believed that applause was an inappropriate response in a baptismal service since they viewed baptism as a time of solemn dedication. These Christians were weaker Christians according to our understanding of Paul's discussion on disputable matters. On the other hand, the evangelistic team felt free to clap with joy at a baptismal service. They were the strong Christians in this instance. How should this situation have been handled according to the principles discussed in this book?

Putting aside the decision-making process of the leaders, the evangelistic team had the responsibility to defer to the weaker Christians in the group. The team needed to give up the action of clapping and to respond with good attitudes. Though the team agreed not to clap anymore, they struggled with their attitudes. It was hard for them not to be critical of the decision of the leadership and the opinions of the weaker Christians. The team was free to disagree with the decision, but they were also responsible to maintain an attitude of oneness by lovingly giving up their right to clap at the service. A good attitude might have enabled them to think of some creative alternatives. For example, they could have had a private reception for the baptismal candidates after the service in someone's home and expressed their joy there.

This clapping incident is representative of the myriads of occasions which call for the application of this book's principles. Other issues that continue to be hotly debated in certain Christian circles are whether or not Christians should date, the way pledge cards and other similar commitments requiring signatures relate to injunctions against rash vows, or whether Christians should borrow money for any purchase such as a loan on a house or for building facilities for a church. The list goes on and on.

But what do we put on the list? The very nature of a disputable matter usually involves some disagreement over whether the issue is essential or nonessential. The weak Christian may feel the issue is essential since it is a moral issue for the weak. The strong Christian will probably disagree. How do we decide whether an issue is neutral?

Five guidelines were suggested in chapter 1. The first guideline for making a decision was whether or not we find a direct scriptural statement or command. Though this guideline seems straightforward, the tendency for some Christians is to hunt for verses that may be remotely related to the issue in order to justify their opposing viewpoint. This approach sometimes escalates the conflict to a point where each side clobbers the other side with Scripture verses. The problem for both sides is that none of the verses used provides a specific, direct statement; otherwise the issue should not be so hotly disputed.

The last of the five guidelines might be helpful in some disputes. If a Christian is willing to die for his or her opinion as the conviction all Christians everywhere should hold, then perhaps the issue is essential, especially if it passes the test of the rest of the guidelines. For me, my list of essentials has become much shorter than it used to be.

Whatever the issue may be, Christians need to develop skills in responding to one another in ways which build up the body of Christ. Neutral issues which cause disruption in relationships require careful handling using the biblical principles presented in this book.

One of the most fundamental principles involves the ability of every Christian to discern whether they are weak or strong in relation to a specific neutral thing. Christians who are unaware of their own weakness on an issue could be endangering themselves and others. The danger to themselves is the possibility that they might sin against their own conscience. Sin against others occurs when they express their opinion in order to impose their conviction on someone else. Many well-meaning but weak Christians quickly slip into the sin of judging others. When this happens, weak Christians can become legalistic and sometimes dogmatic, intolerant, and opinionated.

In disputable matters, the strong Christian also encounters difficulties. Strong Christians need to know who they are because the Bible puts the burden of responsibility on the strong to give up their rights in a dispute over a neutral issue. In addition, strong Christians need to work through their attitude toward the weak. In the clapping incident mentioned above, the strong Christians on the evangelistic team reacted with anger when they were told they could not applaud in the baptismal service. Just as the weak can become critical and judgmental, so also the strong can sin in the same way.

The strong should enjoy their liberties as long as they have no doubts about the issue and are not causing problems for others. If the strong learn that another Christian nearby is weak, the strong should lovingly give up their freedom for the sake of the weak. The strong should also welcome relationships with those who are weak, even those who are legalistic. Normally, if a strong Christian chooses not to do battle with the legalistic Christian, the relationship can continue unhindered. Strong Christians choose their battles wisely. If the strong Christian chooses to ignore legalistic condemnation and express Christian liberty anyway, the strong will need to be ready to suffer some consequences.

One case where the battle may be worth it is in relation to evangelistic strategies. In order to win people to Christ, it may be necessary to take the criticism from legalistic Christians. Strong Christians make the best evangelists and the best missionaries because the freedom of strong Christians enables them to make cross-cultural adjustments.

Another important context for wise application of these principles is in the Christian home. Children need the protection of rules and standards when they are young. In relation to neutral things, Christian parents often have personal convictions which they teach their children, and these parents expect their children to adopt those same convictions. When children become teenagers and begin to think through these issues for themselves, disagreement with parents is to be expected. Wise, mature parents will teach their kids the biblical principles discussed in this book and then allow their budding young adults to come to their own decision on neutral things.

One of the difficulties in disputable matters is what to say to someone when they react to an issue in normal conversation, and we suspect they may be a weaker Christian on that issue. Several steps should be taken in the conversation to communicate love and sensitivity and to allow the person to voice their concern. This approach is a suggested model.

First, be alert to the reactions. Some people can discuss disputable matters with conviction but no overreaction. In such cases you can have a profitable discussion of the issues with logical reasoning. Sometimes people react to an issue with an obviously strong feeling or argumentative spirit. Sometimes you can detect inappropriate responses such as loud, boisterous talking or joking, or perhaps the person becomes unusually quiet. If the person overreacts in these ways, then you must ignore the issue and approach the person with sensitivity to their emotions.

Second, acknowledge their strong feelings. When they overreact, especially if they have become very quiet, make a statement like this, "You seem to have some strong feelings about this." Simple reflection of their feelings may open a floodgate of emotions they need to vent.

Third, look for past, unresolved hurt. Someone who is very opinionated may not be aware that past events have created forcefully entrenched emotions. You might ask something like, "When or how did this develop as a conviction for you?"

Help people identify some past event. Ask them if this particular conviction caused them conflict in the past. Ask how they felt at the time. When you encourage the weak Christian to verbalize feelings and to identify the events which led to those feelings, the individual might begin to calm down enough to have better attitudes toward others who disagree with them. Then you may be able to discuss the issues.

As you read this book, you may have wondered whether the weak has any responsibility to change. You might have felt that the sole responsibility is on the strong and that this whole approach somehow enables the weak to continue being weak. The Bible clearly puts the responsibility on the strong in disputable matters, but those who understand what it means to be weak in disputable matters inherently know that the position of the weak needs to be changed. The term *weak* itself suggests a less than desirable status. Christians who are weak in faith and conscience need to study, learn, and gain knowledge of their freedom in Christ.

Knowledge may be enough, but as we have learned in 1 Corinthians 8, knowledge is not enough for some. Weak Christians should also trust the Lord to give them full liberty of heart and mind. We need to be patient and allow the Holy Spirit to bring about the inner change that is necessary. Even Peter's blanket had to be supernaturally lowered from heaven three times accompanied by a direct word from God before he began to understand he was free to fellowship with Gentiles. We shouldn't be surprised if some Christians struggle to be free. Sometimes, however, the change might occur when the Christian steps out in faith and acts on what is true. Though the Lord never asks anyone to if it means it would be sin for that person, the Lord does want weak Christians to believe they are free to participate without sin.

Whatever our personal conviction may be on a given issue, whether we are weak or strong, each one of us has the responsibility to move toward Christian freedom in nonessentials and to have Christlike attitudes toward one another when we disagree. Until the Lord grants freedom to our weaker friends and family members, the strong will need a good attitude while shouldering the responsibility for the relationship on those issues. We are free to disagree when we have attitudes which develop the unity which pleases God.